The Qur'an and Sayings of Prophet Muhammad

Books in the
SkyLight Illuminations Series

The Qur'an and Sayings of Prophet Muhammad

Selections Annotated & Explained

Annotation by Sohaib N. Sultan

Translation by Yusuf Ali
Revised by Sohaib N. Sultan

Foreword by Jane I. Smith

L.C.C.C. LIBRARY

Walking Together, Finding the Way®
SKYLIGHT PATHS®
PUBLISHING
Woodstock, Vermont

The Qur'an and Sayings of Prophet Muhammad:
Selections Annotated & Explained

2007 First Printing
Annotation and introductory material © 2007 by Sohaib N. Sultan

Yusuf Ali translation of the Qur'an taken from *The Holy Qur'an: Original Arabic Text with*
English Translation & Selected Commentaries, by 'Abdullah Yusuf Ali (Kuala Lumpur, Malaysia:
Saba Islamic Media, 2000). Ali's translation is also widely available online.

All rights reserved. No part of this book may be reproduced or transmitted in any
form or by any means, electronic or mechanical, including photocopying, recording,
or by any information storage and retrieval system, without permission in writing from
the publisher.

For information regarding permission to reprint material from this book, please mail or
fax your request in writing to SkyLight Paths Publishing, Permissions Department,
at the address / fax number listed below, or e-mail your request to permissions@
skylightpaths.com.

Library of Congress Cataloging-in-Publication Data
Sultan, Sohaib.
  The Qur'an and sayings of Prophet Muhammad : selections annotated & explained /
annotation by Sohaib N. Sultan.
    p. cm.
  Includes bibliographical references.
  ISBN-13: 978-1-59473-222-5 (quality pbk.)
  ISBN-10: 1-59473-222-1 (quality pbk.)
  1. Islam—Doctrines. 2. Islam—Essence, genius, nature. 3. Koran—Theology.
  4. Religious life—Islam I. Title.

BP165.5.S85 2007
297.1'227—dc22

2007001915

10 9 8 7 6 5 4 3 2 1

Manufactured in the United States of America

Cover design: Walter C. Bumford III

Cover art: *Holy Qur'an & Islamic Beads*, by Karim Hesham, courtesy of www.istockphoto.com

SkyLight Paths Publishing is creating a place where people of different spiritual traditions come together for challenge and inspiration, a place where we can help each
other understand the mystery that lies at the heart of our existence.

SkyLight Paths sees both believers and seekers as a community that increasingly transcends traditional boundaries of religion and denomination—people wanting to learn
from each other, *walking together, finding the way*.

SkyLight Paths, "Walking Together, Finding the Way" and colophon are trademarks of
LongHill Partners, Inc., registered in the U.S. Patent and Trademark Office.

Walking Together, Finding the Way®
Published by SkyLight Paths® Publishing
A Division of LongHill Partners, Inc.
Sunset Farm Offices, Route 4, P.O. Box 237
Woodstock, VT 05091
Tel: (802) 457-4000   Fax: (802) 457-4004
www.skylightpaths.com

I dedicate this book to
my parents for their love,
my sister and brother-in-law for their encouragement,
my teachers for their wisdom,
my wife for her patience and compassion.

Contents □

Foreword ☐

Jane I. Smith

"Islam does not support violence, but is a religion of peace." "The Qur'an does not condemn Christians and Jews as idolaters, but insists that all who follow the teachings of the Prophets are inheritors of the gardens of paradise." "Muslims do not mistreat women, but consider them to be partners in their families, their communities, and their nations."

In recent years, and particularly since the tragic events of 9/11, Muslims in the West have tried to affirm all of this and much more about the texts and traditions that guide their lives and rule their hearts. Listen, they say, and let us tell you about true Islam, its beauty and its power to give those who would listen to its call a guideline for life and a key to entering into the presence of God. All too often, however, they have not been heard by a broader audience, and citizens of the West continue to ask, What is this Islam that is becoming so visible in our land? What do Muslims really believe, and how can they live with us as fellow citizens in a country far from the traditional heartlands of Islam?

Despite the many efforts to dissociate Islam from movements that support terror and hostility toward the West, fears and misunderstandings are difficult to dispel. Current polls and surveys suggest that prejudice against Islam, Prophet Muhammad, and the Holy Qur'an is not declining but is actually on the rise. As a non-Muslim student and teacher of Islam who is always in search of readable and persuasive presentations about the faith by Muslims themselves, I have been delighted to read this work by my friend and former student Sohaib N. Sultan. I believe it will prove to be a significant contribution to the literature available to the general public on the religion of Islam offered from a personal faith perspective.

Muslims face a formidable task in presenting Prophet Muhammad as not only the vehicle through which the words of God were communicated to humanity and recorded in what we know as the Qur'an, but as the very model for human piety. The history of Christian-Muslim relations has some very bleak aspects, among them the consistent Christian disparaging of the Prophet as a warmonger, a charlatan, and a libertine, and ridicule of the Qur'an as a sadly lacking and misguided attempt to duplicate Jewish and Christian scriptures. This legacy of misunderstanding remains deep in the psyche of the West, and the chore of disentangling it from the good intentions of Christian evangelism or from assumptions implicit in Western foreign policies is formidable.

Meanwhile, Muslims are coming to be a more numerous and more visible presence in America and Western Europe. The last three to four decades in particular have brought new Muslim immigrants to virtually all of the countries of the West. Many Muslim institutions have emerged to help these new citizens struggle to affirm their identity both in relation to their traditional faith and to the nations of which they are now a part. The United States and the countries of Western Europe are responding to this new presence in a variety of ways depending on their respective religious and political heritage. The unfortunate reality that occasional acts of terror continue to be committed by individuals who associate themselves with Islam makes the task of providing a culture of welcome increasingly difficult, exacerbated by sometimes clashing cultural expectations and rising competition for jobs.

America by heritage is a place of greater cultural mix than Europe, and at its best has fostered an ideology of both assimilation and multiculturalism. In reality, however, Muslims, along with many other immigrants arriving on American shores, have not always been welcomed, and have often had difficulty blending into what has been touted as the American cultural melting pot. Immigrant Muslims today also face the difficulty of a challenging American atmosphere of secularism, as well as the necessity of engaging with increasingly large groups of American-born Muslims, including African Americans. In America today Muslims comprise the most diverse, most heterogeneous community to have existed anywhere at any time in the history of the world. It is small wonder that Americans find it hard to know who Muslims really are, what they believe, and how they fit into an already complex American culture.

The task of explaining and interpreting Islam in its many forms, but with its firm foundation in the Qur'an and traditions of the Prophet, is indeed challenging. This book by Sohaib N. Sultan rises to that challenge. The Qur'an in its many English translations, which in reality are attempts at interpretation, is not easy for non-Muslims to grasp or appreciate. Armed with their inherited prejudices, which are often supported by current religious and political rhetoric, westerners find it easy to dismiss the Qur'an and the Prophet of Islam as anachronistic, erroneous, or irrelevant. For the reader not used to its particular style, the text of the scripture itself may be difficult to follow. Sohaib's work helps open the way for both understanding and appreciation of the Holy Qur'an. It provides a narrative of the life and sayings of the Prophet, and the experiences of the early community, that help reveal the integrity of the scripture as it is experienced by the believer.

Many efforts have been put forth recently by Muslims and other scholars of Islam to explain and interpret the beliefs, practices, doctrines, and documents of Islam. Sohaib's rich rendering of the basic texts of the faith is remarkable in a number of ways. He is a deeply devout Muslim, and his comprehension of the Qur'an and the traditions of the Prophet comes from a lifetime of faithful practice. The gentleness and warmth of his own character are revealed in the care with which he opens windows on the text and allows what he understands to be God's own words speak directly to the reader. One is drawn into the text in such a way that he or she works alongside Sohaib to draw out the meaning of each passage. Sohaib has taken traditional Arabic terms and concepts and given them a full and rich treatment that helps convey their meaning in a broad cross-cultural context. He is also a man of this twenty-first century; his style is light and sometimes funny as he lets us know that religion is not antithetical to humor.

This book makes use of several translations of the Qur'an, most notably that of Yusuf Ali. Sohaib's own rendering of the verses he wants to explicate is informed by a deep sense of what they evoke in the heart of the Muslim reader as well as what the words mean in Arabic. The particular genius of this book, however, lies in his careful weaving of Qur'anic text with what we know of the narratives, commentaries, and wisdom sayings of Prophet Muhammad. While students of Islam may learn fairly quickly what it means that Muhammad was the vehicle for the revelation of the Qur'an, and that he was the political leader of a faith that spread rapidly during his lifetime, it takes a bit longer to understand the reverence with which Muslims believe him to be the ultimate example of piety, morality, and wisdom. When people gather together in a house of God to recite the book of God and teach it to one another, according to the Prophet, "Tranquility will descend upon them, mercy will cover them, [and] angels will spread their wings over them." The Qur'an, and the Prophet who sets the context for its understanding in his own life and faith, are presented hand in hand in this deeply sensitive rendering of text and context. Sohaib weaves together the words of scripture and the personality and teachings of the Prophet, helping the reader understand why the *sunnah* (the record of the life and message of Prophet Muhammad) is so crucial to Muslims as the framework within which the Qur'an can be understood.

This book was not specifically written either for or about Islam in the West. Nonetheless it provides a clear and extremely engaging way for the layperson to gain a rich understanding of what animates and motivates Muslims living in Western societies. Neither was it written exclusively for non-Muslims. Persons who have grown up and practiced their faith in Muslim cultures and communities may well find that their appreciation for their Prophet and sacred scripture has been deepened and enriched by this welcoming text. It may provide a very helpful reference for Muslims in the West who are struggling to forge an American Islam in a complex and varied context, with different groups and individuals vying for position as spokespersons and interpreters of the faith. This book tries to set aside those interpretations, which can easily lead to tensions, and takes the reader to the heart of the matter—the heart of the Prophet, the heart of the Qur'an, and the heart of the believer.

Sohaib N. Sultan has earned a reputation for clear thinking and highly readable presentation in his previous book, *The Koran for Dummies*. This book displays the same qualities, along with a gentle invitation to move with him into a deeper interpretation of the Qur'an and *sunnah*. I welcome the reader to an adventure in understanding, not only of the fundamental elements of the faith of Islam but of the most basic convictions of Muslim believers. "Those who patiently persevere in belief and goodness," writes Sohaib, "will be protected and brought to the safe shores of divine presence." He offers the words of the Qur'an and the life of the Prophet as testimony to that promise.

Introduction ☐

For more than 1,400 years the sacred book of Islam, known as the Qur'an, has served as an ocean of wisdom and nourishment for human souls and societies around the world. The Qur'an gave birth to one of the world's most powerful civilizations, which spanned from the depths of Asia and Africa to the heart of Europe. Many historians have even credited the Qur'an for bringing Europe out of the Dark Ages and into the Renaissance with its interwoven ideas of faith and reason, which allowed religion and science to flourish side by side during much of Islamic history. The great historian T. C. Young once wrote, "The great cultural debt we have for Islam since we, Christians, used, within this millennium, to travel to Islamic capitals and to Moslem teachers to learn from them arts, sciences, and the philosophy of human life should always be brought to mind. Amongst this is our classical heritage which Islam preserved in the best way possible until Europe was once again able to understand it and to look after it."[1] Today, Islam's sacred book remains alive not only in the hearts of more than 1.4 billion Muslims across the globe, but also in the beliefs, values, hopes, tensions, and debates that make up our world.

Muslims hold the Qur'an in high esteem as the unaltered word of God revealed to Prophet Muhammad over a twenty-three-year period in seventh-century Arabia. The sacred book was sent down from the heavens in the most marvelous form of Arabic that has ever existed. The striking eloquence of the Qur'an is immediately noticeable because it exists primarily as an oral tradition that is memorized and adorned with the beautiful human voice of recitation. While Muslim theologians consider the Qur'an to be the uncreated word of God—that is, it has always been a part of divine knowledge and therefore was not created by humans—there is no question that the specific context of Arabia and the experiences of Prophet Muhammad's religious community form an essential background for Qur'anic teachings. As such, any good commentary on the Qur'anic passages focuses on the sophisticated meaning of the original Arabic text and considers the historical context in which these passages were first revealed in order to gain deeper insights into the timeless wisdom of the Qur'an.

It goes without saying, then, that Prophet Muhammad's own application and explanation of the Qur'an is seen in Muslim eyes as supplementary guidance to Islam's sacred book. In other words, Prophet Muhammad is, in the words of the Qur'an, "an excellent and beautiful role model for those who long for God, and the last day, and remember God abundantly" (33:21). Prophet Muhammad's wife Ayesha referred to the Prophet as a "walking Qur'an." As such, it is only appropriate to learn the way of Prophet Muhammad in order to delight in the fruitful garden of the Qur'an. The life example of the Prophet is referred to as *sunnah*, and the collections that report his words and deeds are known as *hadith*.

For many people living in the West, teachings of the Qur'an are enshrouded in mystery and fear. Their only exposure to Islam comes via dramatic world events or the media, both of which represent distorted images of the world's second largest religion. This book attempts to present to Western readers the foundational wisdom of Islam that is found in the teachings of the Qur'an and Prophet Muhammad, in an easy-to-understand and easy-to-access manner in order to clarify some of the widespread misperceptions about the Islamic faith. It also endeavors to articulate a vision of Islam that is held and expressed by a vast majority of Muslims. To this end, this work looks at various passages and sayings on essential themes, such as the nature of God and the purpose of human life, and offers short commentaries that reflect general Muslim ideas and concepts and its worldview.

Revelation and Composition of the Qur'an

Muslims believe that the Qur'an is the uncreated word of God that has existed eternally as part of divine knowledge in a "preserved tablet" (Qur'an 85:22). When humanity was ready and in need of the Qur'an, God sent the preserved tablet down to the lowest heavens (*bait al-izza*) in preparation for its revelation through the angel Gabriel to the heart and mind of God's chosen messenger, Prophet Muhammad, passage by passage over a span of twenty-three-years.

This is similar to the Muslim understanding of the Torah of Moses, as well as the Muslim understanding of the Gospel of Jesus. Muslims believe that the original Torah and the original Gospel were also divinely inspired, but that these original revelations were subsequently altered. Hence, when a Muslim refers to the Torah or to the Gospel, he or she may not mean the same thing as the actual texts found in the Hebrew Bible or the Christian New Testament. In this book, when I refer to "the Torah" or "the Gospel," I intend to convey the Muslim understanding of the original revelation. When I mention "the Hebrew Bible" and "the Christian New Testament," I am referring to the actual texts as we possess them today.

The story of the Qur'anic revelation and the beginning of Muhammad's life as a messenger of God began in 610 C.E. while the Prophet was in one of his deep meditations on top of the Mountain of Light (*jabal al-nur*) in a cave known as *hira* in the ancient land of Mecca, which is where Prophet Abraham and Ishmael built the first House of Worship (*kabba*). In the midst of his contemplation, Prophet Muhammad said that a powerful presence suddenly came upon him saying, "Read!" Muhammad, being an illiterate man, was startled by the voice and said, "I do not know how to read." Then the spirit took hold of Muhammad, squeezing him till the Prophet thought he would pass out, and again said, "Read!" Muhammad, shaking and distressed, again repeated his honest claim, "I do not know how to read!" And again the spirit tightly squeezed the Prophet, then let him loose, and recited into Muhammad's ear the first passage of Qur'anic revelation: "Read! In the name of your Guardian-Lord, who created: created humankind from a clot of blood. Read, for your Guardian-Lord is the most generous, who taught by the pen, taught humankind what it did not know" (96:1–5). With the same suddenness with which the spirit appeared, it also left, leaving the new Prophet trembling and unsure of his experience.

Muhammad ran home to the comforting arms of his beloved first wife, Khadija, who wrapped him in a blanket, calmed him down, and asked him what had happened. Upon hearing the Prophet's experience, Khadija took Muhammad for counsel to a learned Christian scholar of scripture by the name of Waraqa ibn Nawfal, who said: "Surely, by the One in whose hand is Waraqa's soul, you are a Prophet of this people. There has come unto you the greatest angel who came unto Moses. Like the Hebrew prophets, you will be called a liar, ill-treated, and they will cast you out and make war upon you." The Prophet was surprised to hear ibn Nawfal's prediction since Prophet Muhammad was a highly respected member of society and referred to by his people as "The Trustworthy" (*al-ameen*). Muhammad asked, "Would my people really drive me out?" Ibn Nawfal replied, "Yes, for no man has come with what you have brought, but was opposed. If I were to live during your era, I would give you great support."

The Christian scholar's prediction came true when Prophet Muhammad began preaching the core Qur'anic message of belief in One God, doing good deeds, social justice, and a Day of Requital when all will have to account for the lives they lived. This message was seen as a threat against the most powerful elements of Arabia because it called for an end to tribal gods of power that claimed dominance over tribes with weaker gods, and it encouraged the fair treatment of the weak—such as the poor, enslaved, orphans, widows, and women—in society. For thirteen years, the Prophet and his community were an oppressed minority in the land until they were forced to migrate to the city of Medina (then known as Yathrib) in 622 C.E., where the next ten years would be spent establishing the first Muslim community. The Prophet's life in Medina would have its own challenges, such as maintaining justice within the community and dealing with constant threats from outside forces hostile toward Islam. During the final year of the Prophet's life, Islam spread in large numbers throughout the Arabian Peninsula, and the Prophet returned to Mecca victorious over his enemies, restoring the House of Worship (*kabba*) to its monotheistic roots.

This general historical background is essential to understanding the context of the Qur'anic passages, which scholars have divided into "Meccan" and "Medinan" verses (*ayah*; pl. *ayat*) depending on whether a passage was revealed in Mecca during the first thirteen years of revelation or revealed in Medina during the latter ten years of revelation. There are 114 chapters (*surah,* pl. *surat*) in the Qur'an, each possessing a specific name (such as "The Opening," "Abraham," "Mary," and so on), that are divided into thirty parts (*juz*) in order to facilitate its reading over a period of a month (one part per night). Eighty-five chapters of the Qur'an were revealed in the Mecca period; twenty-nine chapters were revealed in the Medina period. The "Meccan" chapters are found more toward the middle and end of the book; "Medinan" chapters more commonly appear in the earlier part. Medinan chapters tend to be longer in the number of verses they contain (286 verses being the longest, in chapter 2) and therefore make up about nineteen of the thirty parts in the Qur'an. The Meccan chapters are usually shorter in their number of verses (three verses being the shortest, in chapters 103, 108, and 110) and make up about eleven parts of the Qur'an. The content of typical Meccan passages focuses on affirming the Oneness of God, spiritual devotion, pious conduct, and rewards of the hereafter. Typical Medinan passages continue with these themes but also focus on communal laws, political affairs, business conduct, rules of conflict and resolution, relations with other religious communities, and other such concerns.

The organization of the Qur'an is atypical in that it is not chronological in terms of its revelation or in terms of the stories it relates. Muslims believe that the order of the Qur'an was taught to Prophet Muhammad by the angel Gabriel based on divine instruction. This order was dictated to the scribes of the Prophet and taught to his companions who would then memorize it by heart. During the Prophet's lifetime the Qur'an existed primarily, but not exclusively, as an oral tradition. *Qur'an* literally means "recital" and therefore has always naturally taken the form of recitation, even down to the present day. However, soon after the death of Prophet Muhammad there was a real fear among his companions that if the Qur'an were not collected and preserved in book form (*mushaf*), it would be lost with the companions who had memorized it all by heart. So the first caliph, Abu Bakr, put together a council headed by the most knowledgeable and well-respected of the Qur'an memorizers, Zaid bin Thabit, to have the entire Qur'an written down in the form of a book, which was then checked and authenticated by the memorizers of the scripture.

Later, during the lifetime of the third caliph, Utthman, there was a need to conform the variant recitations of the Qur'an, which existed in seven forms during the lifetime of the Prophet, in order to remove any confusion or division over its "proper" recitation, especially among new Muslims in faraway lands. As such, another council of notable companions was formed to write the Qur'an in a way that conformed to the Prophet's mode of recitation to the exclusion of other forms. Today, all written Qur'an in the form of a book mirror the one put together under the caliphate of Utthman—only twenty years after the Prophet's death—with the only addition being vowel marks (*tashkil*) and diacritical marks (*i'jam*) to facilitate beautiful and correct recitation of the scripture.

Compilation and Form of *Hadith*

For Muslims, the *hadith* serve as an opening into the Qur'an because they give them insight into how the Prophet Muhammad—who is the best of creation in the eyes of Muslims—interpreted and acted on the Qur'an. The Qur'an itself says in several places, "Obey God and the messenger of God" (4:13, for example). Content of the *hadith* consists of wise sayings, commands, prohibitions, deeds, and even matters in which the

Prophet remained silent, which is taken to infer his approval. The *hadith* further clarify and expand upon the sacred law of the Qur'an and are considered second only to the Qur'an in deriving and applying Islamic law (*shariah*). For example, the Qur'an says in several places that Muslims must establish prayer (*salat*) and almsgiving (*zakat*) but offers few details on the hows and whens of these religious laws. It is the *hadith* that contain all the details on how and when to pray and give alms.

Like the Qur'an, the *hadith* existed primarily in oral form with some of Prophet Muhammad's students writing it down. However, during the lifetime of the Prophet, the *hadith*, unlike the Qur'an, did not consist of a body of text that was memorized, and after the death of the Prophet, again unlike the Qur'an, there was no real concerted effort among the companions to put the *hadith* down into book form for preservation and dissemination. This is not to say that *hadith* were not written down by students of each generation, but that *hadith* continued to disseminate in the form of oral tradition from one generation to the next. However, around the eighth century, almost a hundred years after the Prophet's death, scholars felt a real need to collect, authenticate, and write *hadith* down into book form so that they could root out fabricated *hadith* and preserve true *hadith*. These scholars undertook a sophisticated science of discerning true and false *hadith* that is unparalleled in the history of any religious community.

The science of authenticating *hadith* consisted of studying two elements of any given *hadith*: the chain of narration (*isnad*) and content (*matn*). For a *hadith* to be considered authentic there had to be a full chain of narration of trustworthy men and women all the way back to Prophet Muhammad himself. If there was any break in the chain of narration or doubt about the trustworthiness of anyone in the chain going back to the Prophet, then the *hadith* was immediately considered fabricated or given a lesser degree of authenticity. If the chain of narration was complete and everyone in the chain was deemed trustworthy narrators, then the content (*matn*) of the *hadith* was studied. The content had to be consistent with other authenticated sayings of the Prophet and with the teachings of the Qur'an, could not contradict the Qur'an, and had to fulfill many other similar considerations. If the content was sound, along with the chain of narration, then the *hadith* was given full authenticity. Otherwise it was rejected as false or given a lesser degree of authenticity.

An example of the form of a fully authenticated *hadith* is as follows: Malik bin Anas relates from Abu al-Zinnad and Muhammad bin Yahya bin Habban from Al-'Araj from Abu Hurayra that the messenger said, "Let none of you seek a woman in marriage if his brother already is seeking her." Scholars of *hadith* methodology classified all *hadith* that they came across in the oral tradition as "immutably authentic" (*mutwathir*), meaning that the *hadith* was narrated by so many companions that its authenticity was fully agreed upon and its status was equivalent to the status of a verse in the Qur'an; or "fully authentic" (*sahih*), meaning that the chain and content were fully sound and could be used in the codification of law; or "acceptable" (*hasan*), meaning that there was some slight doubt either in the chain or in the content but it was still acceptable enough to be used for codification of law if a *sahih hadith* did not exist; or "weak" (*daif*), meaning that the *hadith* could not be authenticated as being from the Prophet due to a major flaw in the chain or content and therefore could not be used in codification of law, but could still be used to derive general wisdom; or fabricated (*mauda*), meaning that it was definitely not from the Prophet and should not even be used to derive general wisdom because of the potential harm it could cause.

There were many collectors of *hadith* throughout Islamic history and several *hadith* books put together. Eventually though, by the ninth century, there were six collectors of *hadith*—all of Persian heritage from modern day Uzbekistan or Iran—whose books became highly regarded for their diligence in ascertaining the authenticity of *hadith*: Sahih al-Bukhari, collected by Imam Bukhari (d. 870); Sahih Muslim, collected by Imam Muslim (d. 875); Sunan an-Nasa'i, collected by Imam Nasa'i (d. 915); Sunnan Abu Dawud, collected by Imam Abu Dawud (d. 888); Sunnan al-Tirmidhi, collected by Imam Tirmidhi (d. 892); and Sunnan Ibn Maja, collected by Imam Ibn Maja (d. 886). All the *hadith* contained in this book come from these six collections.

Understanding the Essentials of Islam

Having a basic knowledge and understanding of the Islamic faith will make it easier for you to use this book and to navigate the Qur'an and *hadith* on your own. The Arabic word *Islam* comes from the root word *salam*, meaning "peace" and "wholeness." *Islam* itself literally means "surrender" or "submission." Taken as a whole, the religion of Islam can be defined as "Surrendering to God in a state of peace." A Muslim, then, is "One who willingly surrenders to God in a state of peace," and Muslims understand Islam, in this sense, to be the universal religion and path of all previous prophets and believers who are referred to as Muslim in the Qur'an. Islam, as we understand it today, only came as an affirmation and culmination of this universal path, according to Muslim belief. Muslims look to the primary sources of Qur'an and *hadith* to know how best to achieve this state of internal and social peace, and to understand divine will in their lives.

Islam teaches six essential beliefs through its primary sources:

- First is the belief in the absolute Oneness of God without associating any partners. This means that God is the only creator, sustainer, and master of the universe; that all divine attributes are unified in one Supreme Being; and that all worship is due to God alone. God exists in eternity, boundless by time and space, and is therefore the same God that all previous prophets and faith traditions were told to worship and glorify. This is distinct from the Christian doctrine of the Trinity.
- Second is the belief in angels that are created out of light and serve as intermediaries between God and the world by fulfilling certain divine instructions, such as breathing in the spirit of life, recording good and evil deeds, and giving divine revelation or inspiration.

- Third is the belief that God sent prophets throughout history and to all regions of the earth to teach their people about the Oneness of God and the path of surrendering to the will of God. These prophets include all of the prophets mentioned in Jewish and Christian traditions—from Noah and Abraham to Moses and Jesus.
- Fourth is the belief in the books of revelation that all these prophets came with as a means to guide people to the straight path of God. These books include the Scripture of Abraham, the Torah of Moses, the Psalms of David, and the Gospel of Jesus.
- Fifth is the belief in a Day of Requital when everyone will have to answer for the good and evil that they did in the world and be rewarded with paradise or hellfire accordingly.
- Sixth is the belief in divine destiny, meaning that nothing can happen in the universe without the permission, power, and knowledge of God. This takes into account that the free will of human beings exists only with divine permission, and is not independent of God.

There are five pillars in Islam that make up Muslim spiritual practice and devotional life:

- First is bearing witness by the tongue and in the heart that "There is no deity worthy of worship, except God, and Muhammad is the messenger of God." This is the testimony of life for a Muslim, which is renewed at least nine times every day during the prayers. It is rejecting anything or anyone as god other than the One God.
- Second is praying five times a day—before sunrise, at noon, in the afternoon, after sunset, and in the night. The prayer consists of standing, bowing, prostrating, and sitting positions of meditation involving recitation of the Qur'an, mentioning the praises of God, and sending peace and blessings upon all the prophets and their followers.
- Third is the annual giving of alms (*zakat*) from the rich to the poor that consists of a fixed amount based on a person's total wealth. Almsgiving is meant to produce a more generous soul and to create greater justice in society.

- Fourth is fasting during the entire Islamic month of Ramadan—in which the Qur'an was first revealed to Prophet Muhammad—from sunrise to sunset as a spiritual discipline that suppresses the ego of desire and elevates the soul of spiritual devotion and giving. Fasting consists of refraining from food, drink, and any sinful acts, as well as dwelling on unhelpful frames of mind, such as excessive sexual desire, as a way of training the soul in self-restraint and goodness.
- The fifth pillar consists of Muslims going at least once in their lifetime, if they can afford to, on the pilgrimage to the ancient land of Mecca to commemorate the sacred rites established by Prophet Abraham, his son Prophet Ishmael, and wife Hagar. The pilgrimage is thought of as a lifelong journey that washes away sins, purifies the soul, and prepares one for a life of devotion to God.

Islam considers the spiritual and physical elements within a being as complementary entities that require equal attention, rights, and needs. Therefore, the Qur'an and *hadith* contain many teachings on spiritual elevation through self-purification while also stressing that the physical and social rights must be maintained if human societies are to flourish. As such, in Islam you find very rich theological (*aqeeda*), legal (*fiqh*), and spiritual (*ihsan*) traditions that are studied and expounded upon as separate yet deeply intertwined sciences—each building upon the other, and each possessing equal importance. In this book, scholars of *aqeeda* are referred to as "Muslim theologians" when explaining a central point in Islamic theological thought. Similarly, "jurists of Islam" refers to those scholars who specialize in *fiqh*, Islamic law. And, scholars of *ihsan* are referred to as either "people of inward sciences" or "masters of Islamic spirituality." These scholars do not exist in any one school, class, or time period; rather, they are people of different places and time periods who gained prominence in their fields of study among Muslim thinkers and practitioners. In the absence of any hierarchal religious body or priestly class, many scholars gained and continue to gain prominence based as much on their aura and personality as their enlightened teachings.

Living the Qur'an and *Sunnah*

For devout Muslims, the Qur'an and collections (*hadith*) of the prophetic tradition as exemplified by Prophet Muhammad (*sunnah*) are living documents that inform, inspire, and guide their spirituality and morality on a daily basis, from the early morning sunrise to the late hours of the night. When Muslims wake up in the morning to offer their sunrise prayers (*fajr*), they begin with the prophetic example by saying, "All praise is due to God Who restored to me my health and returned to me my soul, and has allowed me to remember the divine" and then recite from a passage in the Qur'an that praises contemplation, belief, and righteousness (3:190–200).

Then they perform a simple physical and spiritual washing known as *wudu* (Qur'an 5:6) just as the Prophet performed it centuries ago. This prepares Muslims for the first of five daily prayers that consists primarily of standing, bowing, and prostrating before God and reciting Qur'anic passages aloud, including the opening chapter of the Qur'an, which is recited at least seventeen times throughout the day. Following prayers, Muslims engage in a personal or collective chanting of divine praise— Glory be to God (*subhan'Allah*), Praise be to God (*allhumdulillah*), God is the Greatest (*Allahu'akbar*), and there is no power other than God's (*la hawla walaa quwata illa billah*) thirty-three or ninety-nine times each— and offer supplication according to Qur'anic instruction and prophetic tradition (2:186).

After beginning the day with spiritual devotion, Muslims set out to partake in the many activities of life, all the while remaining conscious of the scriptural and prophetic counsel that is part of a devout Muslim's consciousness as memorized oral tradition. For example, a Muslim working for the livelihood of his or her family may draw inspiration, by mere remembrance, from the Prophet's words: "Of the wealth you spend in God's way ... the one yielding the greatest reward is that which you spend on your family." Likewise, the Muslim who sets out to seek knowledge may be inspired by the prophetic advice: "Seek knowledge from the cradle to the grave." The Muslim who exercises may seek inspiration from the *hadith*: "your body has a right over you." And, the Muslim who sits down to eat and drink may remind himself or herself of the Qur'anic advice: "O children of Adam … eat and drink, but not excessively, for God loves not those who are excessive" (7:31). The day goes on like this from one activity to another, and in each there is an element of scriptural and prophetic consciousness on the part of a devout believer, which is constantly strengthened through the five daily prayers and other prescribed spiritual practices.

When the night falls, spending time with your family, being intimate with your spouse, and even going to sleep can all be seen as acts of worship when done with the intention of following scriptural and prophetic teachings. Before falling asleep, a Muslim recites from the Verse of the Throne (*ayat al-kursi*) (2:255) and from a passage pertaining to forgiveness and lightening of burdens (2:285–286) to gain divine protection and tranquility while sleeping.

The Qur'an and *sunnah* also act as criteria for how devout Muslims deal with ethical and moral dilemmas on a day-to-day basis concerning issues from business transactions (2:282–283) to gender relations (9:71) to the rights of neighbors (4:36). These passages of scripture—of which there are usually several for any given ethical issue of human concern—offer laws, principles, and insights into what God wants and expects from us in every instance, as well as what we owe God in the way of faith and deeds. Once, there was a mystic and scholar from the city of Baghdad who came across a man drinking alcohol on his way to the mosque. He said to the man, "O servant of God, don't you know that God has proscribed alcohol and prescribed prayer for the believers?" The man spat in his face and insulted him. In response, the scholar said, "And upon you be peace!" The man suddenly felt ashamed for his rudeness and asked the scholar, "From where did you receive such wisdom to behave in this manner?" The scholar replied, "As to my counsel, the Prophet said, 'Religion is based on good counsel' and as to my response to your behavior, God says, 'And the devotees of the Merciful One are those who walk the earth humbly, and when the ignorant address them, they say, 'Peace'" (25:63).

These illustrations convey how central the Qur'an and *sunnah* are in Muslim life—devotional or otherwise. The same can be said of Muslim societies that to this day place much emphasis on helping to cultivate personal aspects of devotion, such as learning proper recitation of scripture, memorizing Qur'anic passages and prophetic traditions, and studying at least the basic teachings of what is contained in them. It is common in Muslim lands to hear Qur'anic recitation coming not only from the mosque at prayer time, but also from the marketplace, radio stations, and television channels. The recitation is beautiful, mesmerizing, and awe-inspiring; those famous for their recitation are elevated to celebrity status in the Muslim world.

It is no surprise, then, that the ideals of the Qur'an and prophetic tradition are highly esteemed in Muslim societies and cultures. The importance of religious practices and values; the hospitality shown toward guests; the culture of sharing food, shelter, and other goods with people; concern for the well-being of young children; high respect for elders; the strong sense of family ties; the emphasis placed on education; the high regard for people of knowledge; and a general sense of goodwill and kindness toward people—all emanate from the teachings of Qur'an and *sunnah*.

This, of course, also means that Muslim societies are constantly looking to the Qur'an and *sunnah* for guidance on the major moral and ethical dilemmas that face them as a culture, such as abortion, the death penalty, organ donation, conditions of war, and so on. The answer is rarely ever clearly spelled out in the Qur'an and *hadith*, but conclusions can be drawn based on general wisdom or reasoning (*illa*) and analogies (*qiyas*) found in these two primary sources.

This process of discerning God's will through the primary sources rarely ever reaches consensus (*ijmaa*) among Islamic scholars, because the richness of the texts leaves room for multiple interpretations. Such differences in opinion can emerge based on: the linguistic study of words within a text and the multiple meanings that can be derived (*lugha*); different understandings of the historical context of a text (*asbab al-nuzul*);

various interpretations on whether a text has a specific ('*aam*) or general (*khaas*) applicability; diverse understandings of the general philosophy of Islamic sciences; and so on. On top of that, every scholar's thoughts and opinions are shaped—whether consciously or subconsciously—by a host of external influences ranging from cultural upbringing to sociopolitical conditions. As such, famous Qur'an and *hadith* commentators throughout history have taken the form of grammarians (such as al-Wahidi, d. 1076), literalists (such as Ibn Kathir, d. 1373), philosophers (such as al-Razi, d. 1209), jurists (such as al-Qurtubi, d.1273), mystics (such as ibn 'Arabi, d.1240), sociopolitical revolutionists (such as Mawdudi, d. 1979), and rationalists (such as Asad, d. 1992) in their primary approach to interpretation. These paradigms of interpretive thought have also produced many different ways of thinking about the Qur'an and *sunnah* in the general Muslim populations of the world. Even Muslims located in one geographical location tend to have vastly different approaches to their religious understandings. There are essential aspects in the teachings of Islam's primary sources—such as absolute belief in One God, a Day of Requital, heaven and hell, daily prayers, almsgiving—that are indisputable and commonly agreed upon. But then there are many matters wherein there is much room for debate and difference of opinion—such as the position of God in the universe, the nature of the afterlife, when war is permitted, how modestly women are required to dress, and much more. This book's focus is on fundamental issues that explain general ideas and concepts in the Qur'an and *hadith*. Teasing out all of the nuances and differences of opinion would distract from that goal, but where appropriate and necessary, I point out different paradigms of interpretation.

Qur'an in the Western Experience

Just as there is no single Muslim experience with the Qur'an, there is no single Western experience of Islam's sacred book. Islam is one of the fastest-growing religions in the West due to migration, birth, and conversion. For many converts, experiencing the Qur'an was what they found most appealing about Islam. For some non-Muslims, too, there is great admiration for the Qur'an, both its beautiful language and its teachings.

Karen Armstrong, a prolific writer on Islam and other world religions, has said, "The bedrock message of the Qur'an is not a doctrine but a simple command that it's right to share your wealth equally, bad to build up a private fortune selfishly, and good to try to create a just and decent society where poor and vulnerable people are treated with respect. That is the bedrock message of the Qur'an, and this is surely what we mean when we talk about decent society and our aspirations in the West."[2] Another admirer of the Qur'an from the West, renowned translator and commentator Thomas Cleary, has written, "One aspect of Islam that is unexpected and yet appealing to the post-Christian secular mind is the harmonious interplay of faith and reason. Islam does not demand unreasoned belief. Rather, it invites intelligent faith, growing from observation, reflection, and contemplation, beginning with nature and what is all around us. Accordingly, antagonism between religion and science such as that familiar to Westerners is foreign to Islam."[3]

At the same time, however, many readers of the Qur'an in the West describe their experience of Islam's sacred revelation as "unconvincingly bland," "artificially pieced together," "difficult to understand," "incoherent babbling," and "uninspiring." These are often descriptions of genuine disappointments that some Westerners have when they first read the Qur'an. This experience may be caused by an underappreciation for the original Arabic language of the text, an encounter with a unique narrative style, a lack of understanding for the historical context of revelation, or the reading of cultural stereotypes into the scripture.

Muslims believe that the beautifully flowing Arabic of the Qur'an can never really be accurately translated into another language for two major reasons. First, translation causes a break in the rhyme, rhythm, and form of the Qur'an that is so brilliantly consistent in its original Arabic even when it speaks of dense subjects like divorce laws or exhilarating themes like the beautiful names of God. The very word *Qur'an* means "recital," and therefore it is meant to be recited out loud, adorned with the beautiful human voice of recitation. The recitation of the Qur'an flows so naturally and perfectly that memorization of its verses becomes almost inevitable after listening to it a few times. Thousands of Muslims memorize the entire 114 chapters of the Qur'an, from beginning to end, and are honored with the title of *hafidhz*, meaning "preserver" of the Qur'an. All Muslims have at least a portion of the Qur'an memorized as a necessary element of the five daily prayers. The aura of the Qur'an exists as a result of its oral nature as a recited book. As such, even the most sincere and excellent efforts at translation can never reproduce the awe Muslims experience upon hearing the Qur'an recited in Arabic. The Western reader of a translated Qur'an misses out on the whole aura of the recital. To experience some of the awe-inspiring beauty, it is well worth it to listen to Qur'anic recitation even if you don't understand a word of Arabic.

Second, the Qur'an is untranslatable because of the richness of the Arabic language in which each word is pregnant with so many meanings that it would take a paragraph to genuinely and accurately translate many of the key terms found in the scripture. Arabic, like Hebrew, is made up of trilateral root letters that impregnate other letters to form a word. Therefore, to fully understand the etymology of any word, it is necessary to examine its trilateral root. For example, the Arabic word *iman* is usually translated into English simply as "belief." But when we examine its trilateral root—*amn*—we find several layers of meaning: "to trust," "to be secure," "to be in safety," "to confine in," "to pledge," "covenant," "faith," and "belief." So, *iman* is more than "belief"; it denotes faith and trust in God and a pledge and covenant to live accordingly. Similarly, when we look at the word opposite *iman*, *kufr*, we see this word usually translated as "disbelief," or "unbelief." But, again, when we examine its trilateral root—*kfr*—we see a host of meanings emerge: "to cover," "to deny," "to hide," "to renounce," "to reject," "to be ungrateful," "negligent," "one who covers the sown seed with earth," "one who conceals the benefit or favor conferred upon him," and "impious." The simple translation of "disbelief" or "unbelief" is inadequate in light of these deeper meanings. *Kufr* is denying and rejecting faith with ingratitude toward God and negligence toward the duties conferred by God, such as telling the truth. The problem with translation is that the vastness and depth of the original Arabic language is lost when it is replaced by words that do not carry the same profundity and may even impart meanings that are alien to the Qur'anic worldview (such as the terms "infidel," "holy war," and others that are used in English but do not appear anywhere in the Qur'anic language).

Another challenge facing the Western reader of the Qur'an is its unique narrative style, structure, and form. The typical Western reader is used to a linear reading of text in which there is clear introduction or beginning, body or middle, and conclusion or ending. The Qur'an is a decisively nonlinear text that has no clear beginning, middle, or end in most of its chapters. The Qur'an is not a story, nor does it follow a storybook narrative. Rather, the Qur'an is a book of guidance that seeks to teach us who God is, what we are expected to do on earth, how we are to live in this world, and what awaits us in the afterlife as we transition from this temporary abode to a more permanent one. Therefore the Qur'an uses a more direct moral narrative in which the reader is addressed in many different ways. Sometimes the Qur'an challenges and confronts the reader with a question: "Where then are you going?" (81:26). Other times the Qur'an will criticize its reader in order to warn against the outcome of selfishness: "You are obsessed by greed more and more until you go down to your graves. Nay, in time you will come to understand!" (102:1–3). And yet, in other places the Qur'an comforts its readers with glad tidings: "Your Guardian-Lord has not left you, and is not displeased. Hereafter will be better for you than the present. Your Guardian-Lord will surely give to you, and you will be content" (93:3–5). The Qur'an uses various tools to address the reader, such as rational arguments, parables, similitude, reminders, and prayers.

Stories of prophets, righteous people, and wicked human beings are told to us within a greater moral narrative as a way of deriving theological, ethical, and spiritual lessons. Therefore, stories are rarely the main focus of an entire chapter in the Qur'an, and details (such as lineage, place, number of years, and so on) are hardly ever mentioned. For example, the story of Adam and Eve is only briefly and partially mentioned in the second chapter (*surah al-Baqara*) and then picked up again and completed in the seventh chapter (*surah al-A'araf*). Similarly, Prophet Moses—the most often mentioned prophet in the Qur'an—is referenced nearly 136 times across thirty-six different chapters whenever his story is of relevance to the greater scriptural message and lesson.

The Qur'an is also nonchronological, meaning that it is not organized from the first revelation sent to Prophet Muhammad to the last one he received. In fact, the first passage revealed to the Prophet is found in Chapter 96, verses 1–5 (*surah al-Iqra*). Rather, Muslims believe that the Qur'an was divinely organized through the angel Gabriel, who taught the order to Prophet Muhammad, who subsequently taught it to his companions, many of whom memorized the whole scripture by heart and some of whom wrote it down as scribes during the Prophet's lifetime and under his supervision. So, passages were revealed to Prophet Muhammad out of order but were then later organized into a complete order by the angel Gabriel during the Prophet's last year of life. When the Qur'an was organized and compiled into book form only a few years after Prophet Muhammad's passing, the written text followed the same structure as the oral recitation.

Due to the unique structure of the Qur'an, it is imperative to read the scripture as a whole, rather than in bits and pieces, so that its teachings are not taken out of their textual contexts. The Qur'an is a self-clarifying book that addresses themes several times over in several different chapters. Therefore, taking one passage about war or women or relations with people of other faiths out of context, without considering other passages on the same theme, can be dangerously misleading and erroneous. This is why I am careful to explain the historical, textual, and thematic contexts of all the themes covered in this book.

A third factor that makes it difficult for many Western readers to appreciate the Qur'an is a lack of historical background about the prevailing conditions during which the Qur'an was revealed to Prophet Muhammad. Much of the Qur'an is a response to events preceding revelation and events occurring during revelation. So, for example, when Qur'anic passages address hostility and fighting with pagan Arabs, it would be a mistake to think that Islam introduced all this fighting to the region. In reality, the pagan tribes of Arabia were engaged in a constant struggle for power and experienced much bloodshed before the advent of Islam. The newly formed Islamic community was responding to this reality, and certain passages in the Qur'an reflect this reality, too. Similarly, when the Qur'an addresses Jews and Christians in a less than friendly way, it is important to go back and study exactly what the Qur'an was responding to at the time of revelation. There we will find that the Qur'an addresses Jews and Christians using tough language only after they had aided the Arab pagans in planning an attack on the Prophet's community in Medina. Otherwise, the Qur'an addresses "People of the Book" in honorable terms, expressing goodwill.

Finally, there is also the fact that Western culture possesses many negative stereotypes about Islam and Muslims in the culture emanating from historical conflicts to present-day tensions. Western readers often see, study, and think about Islam through this lens. For instance, when reading a passage on the inheritance rights of women, Western readers will often focus their attention on the unequal distribution of inheritance between men and women (4:11–12). What they may fail to recognize is that a woman receiving inheritance at all more than 1,400 years ago was inconceivable in other parts of the world, including the West. Furthermore, the Qur'an places all financial obligations for the caretaking of a family upon the male members of a household, while no such obligations are placed on women. As such, the inheritance that women receive remains theirs and only theirs, to be used for whatever they wish. In Islamic history this allowed women to found and endow some major institutions in society. So, while gender bias is read into the Qur'anic rules of inheritance, in reality these rules are based more on gender equity and common sense than any sort of gender discrimination.

The best way for Western readers to overcome all of these barriers to the Qur'an is to read a few general introductory books on Islam, and the Qur'an in particular, in order to become familiar with the common ideas, concepts, and terms that make up the Qur'an. Also, it is beneficial to read multiple translations of the Qur'an at once in order to gain a deeper appreciation for the meaning and vastness of words used in the Qur'an.

Chapters of This Book

This book takes a thematic approach to studying the Qur'an and *hadith* based on selected scriptural passages and prophetic sayings. These selected readings are meant to give a general and broad introduction to the various themes found in Islam's sacred sources. In doing so, some annotation also focus on the key debates and differences of opinion that are found in scholarly interpretation.

Chapters 1 through 6 introduce the most basic elements of the Islamic faith in terms of its teachings on the nature of faith, God, prophets, divine revelation, and the purpose and stages of human life. These chapters focus mostly on theological teachings found in the Qur'an and *hadith* and how they relate to God's relationship with human beings.

Chapters 7 through 10 delve more into the Qur'anic worldview of the self in terms of developing a sound psyche, pure heart, and good character. These chapters will help you understand what the Qur'an teaches us regarding individual spirituality, morality, and responsibility.

Chapters 11 through 15 tackle what may be considered more controversial subjects like religion and society, interfaith relations, issues of war and peace, women's rights, and family concerns. These passages express the content of the Qur'an that has most to do with the social fabric of human civilization.

Exploring these themes will give you an enlightened insight into one of the world's greatest religious traditions and the remarkable piety and devotion of Muslims who simply seek to live their faith out of a sincere love for God. This book will remove certain misconceptions about Islam that are commonly found in the West, and it will at a deeper level help you think anew about the world we live in today. The richness of the Islamic tradition will at once become apparent, causing black-and-white notions of the Islamic faith and Muslim world to whither away.

It is my hope that through this book, readers will be exposed to the teachings, values, and ethics that Muslims around the world hold onto so dearly, and that it will in the end lead to a greater appreciation of our collective heritage and ideals as human beings. What is bound to emerge is a realization of our common heritage as people of faith and a renewed belief in the dialogue of civilizations that will confront the ideology of a clash of civilizations.

A Note on the Translation

Translating the Qur'an is perhaps one of the most difficult tasks in Islamic scholarship because of the sacredness of the original Arabic text and its place in Muslim life. Recognizing this fact, most translators describe their work with the Qur'an as an interpretation, rather than as an actual, literal translation. Translations of the Qur'an into English are constantly evolving, with new translators putting forth new models and ideas in translation.

In this book, I have chosen, for the most part, to use the translation of Yusuf Ali, a famous twentieth-century Indian Islamic scholar (d. 1953) whose work on the Qur'an, first published in 1934, is highly respected among Muslims of all generations for its clarity, fluidity, and depth. Ali's work has passed the test of time in terms of its acceptability as translation that reflects mainstream Islamic thought and Muslim values. His translation is also very accessible and freely available on the Web.

However, no translation is ever perfect, and no two translators think in exactly the same way. Therefore, I have updated Yusuf Ali's original work to language that is more accessible to the modern reader of English. Often I have chosen another word to define a Qur'anic concept that can be translated in many different ways, and I sometimes also restructured sentences for clarity. In such cases, I explain in the annotation the vastness of the meaning of a word and the different implications it holds in interpreting the Qur'an. For example, Yusuf Ali defines the Arabic word *taqwa* in many different ways, such as "God-fearing," that in my opinion give only a partial meaning to the word. Therefore, I have translated *taqwa* in every instance as "God consciousness" as a more comprehensive and accurate meaning.

In my efforts to offer a revised translation, I must acknowledge the great work of two other Qur'an translators whose flexible yet accurate approach to translating the Qur'an influenced my own deliberations. The first is the work of Muhammad Asad, a convert to Islam and one of the most respected Muslim intellectuals of the late twentieth century (d. 1992), who wrote a translation of the Qur'an known as *The Message of the Qur'an*,[4] first published in 1980. Asad's translation is respected for its brilliance in succinctly describing Qur'anic terminology rather than settling for a less accurate word-for-word translation. For example, whereas most translators before Asad were content with translating *kafir* as "unbeliever" or "disbeliever," Asad translated *kafir* as "rejecter of faith." Inspired by this idea, I have often used succinct phrases to translate a single Qur'anic term for greater accuracy and specificity.

The second translation is the brilliant work of Thomas Cleary, a scholar of Eastern languages and civilizations from Harvard University, in *The Qur'an: A New Translation*,[5] first published in 2004. In my opinion, Cleary's translation shows a mastery of both the Arabic and English language that is unprecedented. Cleary has a unique ability to draw from the vastness of the English language in translating the vastness of the Arabic language. This makes Cleary's translation succinct and enjoyable to read. For example, Cleary more accurately translates *yawm al-din* as "the Day of Requital" as opposed to the less accurate, yet more common translation "the Day of Judgment." Following Cleary's lead, I too use "Requital" instead of "Judgment" and have otherwise tried to use more descriptive, but accurate, terms in translation. Also, Cleary's is the first translation that realizes the problem of describing God in the third person as "He" in English, given that Islamic theology gives no room for anthropomorphism. Appreciating this idea, I, too, have avoided using "He" in my revised translation of Ali's work.

Quotations from the Hebrew Bible and Christian New Testament are taken from the New American Standard Bible.

The Qur'an and Sayings
of Prophet Muhammad

1 Proof of God's existence and divine attributes are in every single living creature, from the stars in the high heavens to the ant on earth, each in its own way pointing to the creative genius of a truly awesome Creator. Throughout the Qur'an there are verses that beautifully describe an aspect of the created world, with concluding statements such as, "These are signs for those who think," or with a question such as "Will they then not reflect?" The word "reason" is mentioned 77 times and the word "think" 128 times in the Qur'an. These emphasize the use of our senses to discover God, who is present wherever we turn (Qur'an 2:115).

2 Contemplation, reflection, introspection—all of these have often been mentioned as the beginning point of spiritual guidance and enlightenment in the books of Islamic spirituality. The more you contemplate the signs of God all around you, the more you will find yourself drawing closer to the reality of God's existence and presence in your own life. Interestingly, the postures of meditation mentioned in this passage—standing, sitting, and lying down—are the same meditation postures found in Buddhism, which points to a continuation of certain spiritual practices from previous faith traditions.

3 Through contemplation you are able to access the farthest depths of reason, which will naturally lead you to conclude that God created you and the entire universe for a very real and meaningful purpose, and not for mere entertainment (Qur'an 44:38). "Glory to You" means that the function of the created world is to glorify and worship the Creator (Qur'an 51:56). "Keep us, then, from the torment of the fire" is an acknowledgment on behalf of the enlightened that he or she is an imperfect being and is therefore in need of God's mercy, forgiveness, and aid in order to fulfill life's great purpose.

1 □ On Contemplation, Reason, and Faith

Behold! In the creation of the heavens and the earth, and the alternation of night and day, there are indeed signs for people of understanding[1]— those who celebrate the praises of God, standing, sitting, and lying down on their sides, contemplating the creation of the heavens and the earth[2]: Our Guardian-Lord! You did not create all of this for nothing! Glory to You! Keep us, then, from the torment of the fire![3]

—QUR'AN 3:190–191

Behold! In the creation of the heavens and the earth; in the alternations of the night and the day; in the sailing of the ships through the ocean for the profit of human beings; in the rain which God sends down from the skies, and the life which God gives therewith to a land that is dead; in the beasts of all kinds that God scatters through the earth; in the change of the winds, and the clouds employed between sky and earth, surely there are signs for people that are wise. Yet there are people who take others besides God as equal, loving them as God should be loved.

—QUR'AN 2:164–165

4   The Qur'anic proof for the Oneness of God rests on the argument that the sophisticated order of the heavens and earth suggests that there is One Creator, Sustainer, and Caretaker. If there were more than One God, then the entire universe would be in a constant state of chaos and upheaval, with gods competing against each other for power (Qur'an 23:91).

5   Again the Qur'an appeals to human reason to argue that if there were truly other gods beyond the One God, they would have the capability at least to create something as small and simple as a living fly. Since no such power exists in the heavens or on earth other than God, logic would entail that there is only One God—the One who creates all living things. Therefore nothing in the universe is worthy of glory and worship, except God.

If there were, in the heavens and the earth, other gods besides God, there would have been confusion in both! So Glory to God, Guardian-Lord of the Throne, beyond what they ascribe.[4]

—QUR'AN 21:22

O humanity! Here is a parable set forth, so listen to it: Those on whom, besides God, you call, cannot create even a fly, if they all met together for such a purpose. And if a fly should snatch away anything from them, they would have no power to release it from the fly. Feeble are those who petition and those whom they petition.[5]

—QUR'AN 22:73

And God has subjected to you the night and the day; the sun and the moon; and the stars are subject by the divine order. Verily in this are signs for people who are wise. And the things on this earth which God has multiplied in varying colors and forms; verily in this is a sign for people who celebrate the praises of God. And it is God who has subjected the sea, that you may eat flesh that is fresh and tender, and that you may extract from there ornaments to wear. And you see the ships therein that plough the waves, that you may seek the bounty of God and that you may be grateful. And God has set up on the earth mountains standing firm, lest it should shake with you; and rivers and roads, that you may find your way; and landmarks. And [people] also find their way by the stars. So then is one who creates like one that creates not? Will you not then receive lessons?

—QUR'AN 16:12–17

6 Prophet Abraham, known as the "father of faith" in all three Abrahamic traditions—Judaism, Christianity, and Islam—began his own spiritual journey using contemplation and reason. Abraham could not reasonably accept worshiping man-made idols in the tradition of his father and forefathers, so he set out on a personal quest in search for his God.

✦ "We" is used in the Qur'an to refer to God in the royal, majestic sense. This does not in any way imply the existence of a god other than the One God.

7 As Abraham searched for God in the high heavens he came upon the luminous stars, moon, and sun that have such splendor to them that he thought they might be of divine nature. But every time the object of his adoration would disappear it would leave him searching for a divine being that, if worthy of worship and devotion, would be constant and ever-present. So finally, when the great sun set, Abraham realized that there must be One God who creates and controls all the things he had witnessed in the high heavens and on earth, and therefore it is only this One God who is truly worthy of being his Guardian-Lord (Qur'an 41:37). Interestingly, Abraham goes through the process of negating who and what is not divine before he comes to affirm who and what God is. This corresponds with the Islamic testimony of faith that says, "There is no god, except God" (*la illaha illa Allah*), which also first negates anything and anyone as divine before affirming the reality of the One God.

8 Once Abraham attained to faith and gained certainty in his belief of One God, he dedicated himself firmly and wholly unto God and made a commitment never to obey or serve anything or anyone in place of God. Indeed, this is what faith means and entails. In the story of Abraham we have a model for our own search and discovery of God through contemplation, the use of reason, and finally accepting the reality of what our minds and hearts show us to be true.

And Abraham said to his father Azar, "Do you take idols for gods? I see you and your people in evident error." And so We showed Abraham the power and the laws of the heavens and the earth, so that he would become among those who gain certainty.[6] Then, when the night covered him over he saw a star: he said, "This is my Guardian-Lord." But when it set, he said, "I love not what goes down." Then, when he saw the moon rising, he said, "This is my Guardian-Lord." But when the moon set, he said, "Unless my Guardian-Lord guides me, I shall surely be among those who go astray." Then, when he saw the sun rising, he said, "This is my Guardian-Lord, for this is the greatest." But when the sun set, he said, "O my people! I am indeed free from your giving partners to God.[7] For me, I have set my being firmly and truly toward God Who created the heavens and the earth, and never shall I attribute partners with God."[8]

—QUR'AN 6:74–79

9 Here Prophet Abraham again used reason to argue against idolatry and for the worship of One God. In breaking the idols to pieces, Abraham made his people think introspectively about what they were worshiping and serving—gods without any power, speech, or hearing. In our times, we, too, find ourselves surrounded with idols that are glorified and loved more than God, such as wealth, nationality, and, most commonly, our own lower desires. These, like the idols of Abraham's people, are human-made entities that can neither hear nor speak, and they only possess power to help or hurt us insofar as we attribute such power to them. Breaking our addiction to these idols gives us the freedom to lovingly and willingly serve the only One worthy of worship and devotion.

10 One of the greatest obstacles to attaining faith is a false sense of self-sufficiency and power. In such a condition, it is difficult for us, like the king in this story, to even listen to voices of reason. And the more the ego is allowed to grow in its arrogance, the more we become distant from divine guidance. For this reason, Muslim scholars have said that sincerity, true longing for faith, and self-purification from spiritual ailments are a must in order to receive enlightenment. This concept is similar to the Buddhist philosophy that spiritual awakening can only occur if we are willing to confront our own delusion of independent existence.

We bestowed aforetime on Abraham right conduct, and well were We acquainted with him. Behold, he said to his father and his people, "What are these images to which you are so devoted?" They said, "We found our fathers worshiping them." Abraham said, "Indeed you have been in manifest error—you and your fathers." They said, "Have you brought us the truth or are you one of those who jest?" Abraham said, "Nay, your Guardian-Lord is the Guardian-Lord of the heavens and the earth, Who created them, and I bear witness to this. And by God, I have a plan for your idols after you go away and turn your backs." So [Abraham] broke [the idols] to pieces except for the largest one so that [the people] might turn to it. They said, "Who has done this to our gods? He must indeed be some man of impiety!" They said, "We heard a youth talk of them, he is called Abraham." They said, "Then bring him before the eyes of the people so that they may bear witness." They said, "Are you the one that did this with our gods, O Abraham?" Abraham said, "Nay, this was done by their biggest [idol]; ask [the idols] if they can speak intelligently!" Then were they confounded with shame: "You know full well that these [idols] do not speak." Abraham said, "Do you then worship besides God things that can neither be of any good to you nor do you harm? Fie upon you, and upon the things that you worship besides God! Will you not, then, use your reason?"**9**

—QUR'AN 21:51–67

Have you not turned your attention to one who disputed with Abraham about his Guardian-Lord, because God had granted him power? Abraham said, "My Guardian-Lord is one who gives life and death." [The king] replied, "I give life and death." Said Abraham, "But it is God that causes the sun to rise from the East, can you then cause it to rise from the West?" Thus the rejecter of faith was confounded, for God does not grant guidance to unjust people.**10**

—QUR'AN 2:258

11 In this story, which is shared among the three Abrahamic faiths, Prophet Abraham and his son show us what it truly means to be a faithful devotee of God, and what it means to willingly surrender your will unto God: It means placing God's will over your own will, wants, and desires; and it means being willing to sacrifice what is most near and dear to you for the sake of God. This may mean sacrificing such things as material possessions, fame, and lower desires, if those things take you away from nearness to God, and fulfillment of religious duties (Qur'an 3:92). Abraham was put through a trial that most of us would have failed, but in passing the test he reached the highest level of faith and was adorned with the title "The Friend of God" (*khaleel ul-Allah*) (4:125).

12 This verse was revealed in response to the Jews and Christians of Arabia who argued with Prophet Muhammad, saying that a person had to be a Jew or Christian to be rightly guided. The rebuttal offered here is that Prophet Abraham, whom all three faiths recognize as being rightly guided, was sent to humanity before the advent of Judaism or Christianity, and therefore must have been neither a Jew nor a Christian. So the question that this passage seeks to answer is, what was the path and religion of Abraham?

13 Abraham was a *haneef,* meaning he naturally inclined toward that which was true and good based on the predisposed nature of the heart to recognize truth and goodness; and he turned away from anything false and evil.

14 Abraham was a *muslim,* meaning that he willingly surrendered his will to God, committing himself to the path of loving worship to the One God. When the Qur'an describes Abraham as a *muslim,* it does so seeking to reclaim the universality of Abraham as the model for all those who believe in One God and willingly surrender themselves to divine will (Qur'an 60:4–6). Therefore, Muslims do not consider Islam to be a new religion; rather Muslims consider the way of Islam (surrender to God in a state of peace) to be the way of all prophets and their followers, from Adam all the way down to Muhammad. The teachings of Prophet Muhammad are simply an affirmation and culmination of this universal way, according to Muslim belief.

[Abraham prayed] "O my Guardian-Lord! Grant me a righteous progeny." So We announced joyful news to him of a good-natured son. Then when [the son] had come of age to work together, [Abraham] said, "My son, I see in a dream that I sacrifice you. Now let's see what you think." [The son] said, "Father, do what you are commanded, you will find me, God willing, bearing it calmly." Then when both had willingly surrendered their will to God and [Abraham] lay him down, on his forehead, We called to him, "Abraham! You have already fulfilled your vision." For that is how We reward those who do good; for this was certainly an evident trial, as We redeemed him through a tremendous sacrifice, and We left for him in future generations. Peace upon Abraham! That is how We reward those who do good; for he was one of Our faithful devotees.[11]

—QUR'AN 37:100–111

Abraham was not a Jew nor yet a Christian;[12] but he was true in faith [*haneef*],[13] and willingly surrendered his will to God (*muslim*),[14] and he joined not gods with God.

—QUR'AN 3:67

15 Faith and righteous deeds go hand in hand; one is deficient without the other. Everywhere in the Qur'an faith is always attached to doing good deeds, and vice versa. Having faith and trust in God means fulfilling divine commandments, which at its core requires doing good works that benefit your own soul and the people around you. Thus, Prophet Muhammad said, in what is considered to be the golden principle of Islam, "None of you truly believes until he loves for his brother what he loves for himself." The same ethic is mirrored in Judaism: "Love your neighbors as yourself" (Leviticus 19:18); and in Christianity: "Do unto others as you would have them do unto you" (Luke 6:31).

Verily this recital does guide to that which is most upright, and give glad tidings to the believers who do deeds of righteousness, that they shall have a great reward.[15]

—QUR'AN 17:9

Say: "Verily, my Guardian-Lord has guided me to a Way that is straight—a religion of right—the path of Abraham the true in faith, for he joined not gods with God." Say: "Truly, my prayer and my service of sacrifice, my life and my death, are for God, the cherisher of the worlds. No partner has God; this am I commanded, and I am the first of those who surrender to God's will."

—QUR'AN 6:161–163

Do they seek something other than the religion of God—while all creatures in the heavens and on earth have, willing or unwilling, surrendered to God's will, and to God shall they all be returned? Say: "We believe in God, and in what has been revealed to us and what was revealed to Abraham, Ishmael, Isaac, Jacob, and the Tribes, and in what was given to Moses, Jesus, and the prophets, from their Lord. We make no distinction between one and another among them, and we surrender our will to God."

—QUR'AN 3:83–84

1 The term for "God" in Arabic is Allah, a beautiful word that literally translates into "The God" or "The Object of Adoration." By its very linguistic nature, it cannot be pluralized (in the way God can be pluralized into gods) or take the form of gender (in the way God can be turned into goddess). Therefore, the very theological nature of Allah is Oneness and unique beyond gender—male or female. The Qur'an sometimes refers to God in the third person, using *huwa,* which is usually translated as "He" in English. But in this book I refrain from using the word "He" to refer to God because it gives an inaccurate concept of the nature of God in Islamic theology. The Qur'an also refers to God in the first-person "I" (2:186, for example), second-person "You" (1:5, for example), and royal-person "We" (41:31, for example).

2 Every chapter in the Qur'an begins with this invocation to remind the noble reader of God's preeminent attributes: Mercy (*rahman*) and Compassion (*raheem*). Both of these words are linguistically related in their common root word *rahm,* which means "womb." Therefore *rahman* and *raheem* are rooted in mother-like mercy and compassion. Muslim theologians say that Mercy is an attribute of God's being, while Compassion is divine expression or manifestation of mercy in the created world. As such, this invocation is also commonly translated as "In the name of God, the Merciful, the Mercy-giving."

2 □ On God and Divine Attributes

By the name of God,[1] the Merciful, the Compassionate.[2]

—QUR'AN 1:1

O son of Adam, so long as you call upon Me and ask of Me, I shall forgive you for what you have done, and I shall not mind. O son of Adam, were your sins to reach the clouds of the sky and were you then to ask forgiveness of Me, I would forgive you. O son of Adam, were you to come to Me with sins nearly as great as the earth, and were you then to face Me, I would bring you forgiveness nearly as great.

—DIVINE SAYING RELATED BY PROPHET MUHAMMAD

3 The "Pure Truth" (*Surat al-Ikhlas*) is one of the shortest chapters in the Qur'an, and yet its message on the absolute oneness and uniqueness of God makes it one of the most celebrated and most often read passages in Muslim circles. In fact, Prophet Muhammad said that this short chapter represents one-third of the Qur'an in terms of the centrality of its teachings. From "It is the One God," Muslims are taught to believe in absolute monotheism and to declare in their testimony of faith that "There is nothing worthy of worship, except God."

4 The divine attribute of *samad* is translated here as "the Eternal, the independent cause of all being." However, *samad* is a difficult word to translate because it has a vast meaning that encompasses the idea of God as self-sufficient and existing independently of anyone or anything, while all else is utterly dependent on God for sustenance and existence.

5 Here, Muslims find a negation of any notion that God was born or has any children. Rather, God is pre-eternal with no mother, father, son, or daughter.

6 Finally, God's Uniqueness means that there is no other being that can be compared with God, and therefore God exists outside of any physical concept that the human mind may conceive of. In other words, there is no room for anthropomorphism in Islamic theology. As such, Muslims are forbidden from making any graven images of God, which is consistent with the second of the Ten Commandments in the biblical books of Exodus and Deuteronomy.

7 This verse is known in Muslim circles as the "verse of the throne" (*ayat al-kursi*), due to its powerful description of God's all-encompassing Power, Knowledge, and Majesty. In the tradition of Prophet Muhammad, Muslims recite this verse to invoke God's protection before leaving the home, traveling on a journey, going to sleep, and so on. The verse especially produces a sense of awe for the divine when chanted in Arabic.

Say, "It is the One God.³ God, the Eternal, the independent cause of all being.⁴ Neither gives birth, nor was ever born.⁵ And there is nothing comparable unto God."⁶

—QUR'AN 112

God—there is no god but God! The Living, the Self-subsisting, Supporter of all, whom neither slumber nor sleep can overtake. To God belongs what is in the heavens and what is on earth. Who intercedes with God, except by divine permission? God knows what is before them, and what is after them; but they do not encompass anything of that knowledge, except as God wills. The throne of God extends over the heavens and the earth, whose preservation does not fatigue God, who is truly Exalted, the Supreme.⁷

—QUR'AN 2:255

Whatever is in the heavens and on earth, let it declare the praises and glory of God, for God is the Exalted in Might, the Wise. To God belongs the dominion of the heavens and the earth; it is God who gives life and death; and God has power over all things. God is the First and the Last, the Evident and the Immanent, and God has full knowledge of all things.

—QUR'AN 57:1–5

No son did God beget, nor are there any coexistent deities, [for if there were other gods,] behold, each god would have taken away what it created, and some of them would surely gain ascendancy over others. God is beyond anything they describe. God knows what is hidden and what is manifest; too sublime is God for the partners they attribute!

—QUR'AN 23:91–92

8 This passage mentions many of God's most beautiful names (*asma' ul-husna*) of which there are ninety-nine in the Islamic tradition. These names are a way for the created to know and to relate to the Creator. The attributes of God are divided into two categories: the Majestic (*al-jalal*) and the Beautiful (*al-jamal*). The Majestic qualities relate to divine transcendence, such as the Powerful, the Holy, and the All-Knowing. The Beautiful attributes relate to divine imminence, such as the Forgiving, the Kind, and the Loving. The division of these attributes allows Muslims to conceive of God as both above humanity, in the position of master or ruler, and as near humanity, in the position of friend and beloved. Each divine attribute is meant to evoke deep contemplation in the heart, and such reflection is often done alone or in group settings through chanting of the names. Prophet Muhammad once said that "God has ninety-nine names and whoever enumerates them will enter paradise."

9 This is an excellent example of the type of metaphor sometimes used in the Qur'an to describe the beauty and perfection of God. For many Qur'anic commentators, the metaphor of a glass enclosing a lamp inspires an image of spiritual illumination (lamp) that takes place within the hearts (glass) of God's devotees. For all interpreters this verse is a description of God's eternal and universal light by which humanity discovers and experiences spiritual illumination.

10 Some of the attributes given to God may give the idea of divine transcendence to the exclusion of divine imminence. However, this verse makes it clear that the Qur'anic concept of God is one in which the divine has a close, intimate relationship with human beings. In a divinely revealed *hadith,* Prophet Muhammad relates that God says, "I am as My servant thinks of Me. I am with him when he makes mention of Me. If he makes mention of Me to himself, I make mention of him to Myself; and if he makes mention of Me in an assembly, I make mention of him in an assembly better than it. And if he draws near to Me a hand's length, I draw near to him an arm's length. And if he comes to Me walking, I go to him running."

It is God, other than Whom there is no other god. Who knows all things hidden and open, who is the Merciful, the Compassionate. It is God, other than Whom there is no other god. The Sovereign, the Holy, the Source of Peace, the Guardian of Faith, the Preserver of Safety, the Exalted in Might, the Omnipotent, the Overwhelming. Glory to God, beyond any association they attribute. It is God, the Creator, the Originator, the Fashioner—to God belong the most beautiful names. Whatever is in the heavens and on earth celebrate God's praises and glory, Who is Exalted in Might, the Wise.[8]

—QUR'AN 59:22–24

God is the Light of the heavens and the earth. The parable of divine light is as if there was a niche and within it a lamp; the lamp enclosed in glass; the glass as it were a shining star; lit from a blessed olive tree, neither of the East nor of the West, whose oil is well-nigh luminous even without fire touching it. Light upon light: God guides whom God wills to divine light. God sets forth parables for men, and God does know all things.[9]

—QUR'AN 24:35

When My servants ask you concerning Me, I am indeed near. I respond to the prayer of every supplicant when he calls on Me. Let them also, with a will, listen to My call, and believe in Me, so that they might follow the right way.[10]

—QUR'AN 2:187

11 Of course, the beauty referred to here is inner beauty and beautiful deeds, because Prophet Muhammad also teaches that "God does not look to your outward appearance or your wealth, but rather to your heart and deeds."

When God created the creation, God wrote in the book, which is with God over the divine Throne: "Verily, My Mercy surpasses My Wrath."

—PROPHET MUHAMMAD

God is Beautiful and loves beauty.[11]

—PROPHET MUHAMMAD

What God out of divine mercy does bestow on humankind there is none that can withhold; [and] what God does withhold, there is none that can grant, apart from God; and God is the Exalted in Power, full of Wisdom. O humanity, call to mind the grace of God unto you! Is there a Creator, other than God, to give you sustenance from heaven or earth? There is no god but God. How then are ye deluded away from the Truth?

—QUR'AN 35:2–3

God is the one that accepts repentance from God's servants and forgives sins, and God knows all that ye do.

—QUR'AN 42:25

God is never unjust in the least degree. If there is any good [done], God doubles it, and gives from divine presence a magnificent reward.

—QUR'AN 4:40

◆ Revelation, in the Islamic tradition, is what comes down from God to prophets or messengers via angelic beings. For prophets, revelation entails guidance on what to say and how to act in any given situation in accordance with divine will. For messengers revelation also entails receiving a scripture that contains moral teachings and laws for human beings. Revelation should not be confused with divine inspiration (*ilham*), which even pious nonprophets can receive, such as the wise man by the name of Luqman (Qur'an 31:12–19), and which never ceases to end. Indeed, divine inspiration also comes to the nonhuman created world, such as the community of bees mentioned in the Qur'an (16:68). As such, revelation is a unique and distinct form of communication between God and human beings that was only given to prophets or messengers, with Adam being the first and Muhammad being the last, according to Muslim belief. In terms of revealed scriptures, the Torah given to Moses, the Psalms bestowed on David, the Gospel of Jesus, and the Qur'an sent to Muhammad are all mentioned by name. There is a mention of the scrolls of Abraham (Qur'an, 87:19), but no particular name or description is given to this revelation.

1 From the very beginning of time, humanity has received revelatory guidance from above as a means to access divine will and instruction for earthly life. Here Adam, the first human being, is given guidance and told that the ones who follow it will only benefit their own souls, and those who reject and go astray from it will only harm their own souls. The same is said about the Qur'anic guidance that came to Prophet Muhammad in several other passages (39:41, for example). So, we can conclude from this that the primary purpose of divine revelation is to guide human life to the path of God.

3 □ On Revelation and Scripture

[And after Adam disobeyed and fell into error] his Sustainer chose him and turned to him, and gave him guidance: "Get down from there, both of you, all together, from the garden with enmity between some. But if, as is sure, there comes to you guidance from Me, whosoever follows My guidance will not lose his way, nor fall into misery. But whosoever turns away from My reminder, verily for him is a life narrowed down, and We shall raise him up blind on the Day of Resurrection."[1]

—QUR'AN 20:122–124

We did send messengers before you, and appointed for them wives and children. And no messenger could bring a sign but by permission of God. There is a scripture for every era.

—QUR'AN 13:38

None of Our revelations do We abrogate or cause to be forgotten, but We substitute something better or similar: know you not that God hath power over all things?

—QUR'AN 2:106

2 | Here the "you" is understood to mean Prophet Muhammad since he was the one who received the Qur'an as revelation.

3 | The Qur'an never claims to have brought a new message and a new religion for people to follow. Rather, the Qur'an says that it is a reminder and an affirmation of the sacred truths found in previously revealed scriptures.

4 | The Torah of Moses and the Gospel of Jesus are mentioned here as scriptures that were sent by God for the purpose of guidance. As such, Muslims are required, by faith, to believe in the unaltered, original Torah and Gospel as books of revelation. However, emphasis must be placed on the word "original" because Muslims believe that the Torah and Gospel were altered by the hands of men in later generations.

5 | "Criterion" is another word used to describe revealed scriptures, and one of the names given to the Qur'an (al-furqan). For Muslims scripture represents the criterion that allows believers to distinguish between truth and falsehood, good and evil. Implicit in this belief is a rejection of moral relativism in which all moral opinions or conclusions are equally valid. Instead, for Muslims, the way to know truth and goodness is through a reflective study of scriptural teachings.

6 | Meaning that those who reject the teachings of scripture in reality abandon life's very purpose and thus return to God with an unfulfilled life. The key word here is "reject," because it implies an active form of rebelling or turning against God's instructions and path. It is the active rejection of faith that is reprehensible and deserving of retribution, according to the Qur'an.

It is God who sent down to you,**2** in truth, the book confirming what went before it;**3** And God sent down the Torah and the Gospel before this, as a guide to humanity,**4** and God sent down the criterion.**5** Then those who reject the signs of God will experience a severe retribution, for God is exalted in might, Lord of retribution.**6**

—QUR'AN 3:3–4

We gave Moses the book and followed him up with a succession of messengers. We gave Jesus the son of Mary clear proofs and strengthened him with the Holy Spirit. Is it that whenever there comes to you a messenger with what you yourselves desire not, you are puffed up with pride? Some you called impostors, and others you slay!

—QUR'AN 2:87

We appointed for Moses thirty nights, and completed them with ten more; thus the term with his Lord was completed in forty nights. And Moses had charged his brother Aaron: "Act for me amongst my people, do right, and follow not the way of those who do mischief." When Moses came to the place appointed by Us, and his Lord addressed him, he said: "O my Lord! Show [Yourself] to me, that I may look upon you." God said: "By no means can you see Me, but look upon the mountain— if it remains in its place, then you will see Me." When his Lord manifested to the mountain, that caused [the mountain to crumble] into dust, and Moses fell down in awe. When [Moses] recovered his senses he said: "Glory be to You! To You I turn in repentance, and I am the first to believe." [God] said: "O Moses! I have chosen you over the people by My mission and by My word. Take then what I have given you, and be of those who are grateful."

—QUR'AN 7:142–147

7 "Light" is another description given to revealed scripture, here specifically to the Torah, but in other passages to the Gospel of Jesus (5:46) and the Qur'an (5:15). The nature of light in relation to revelation is very interesting: light is what extinguishes darkness, or we can say that darkness is simply the absence of light. In the same way, moral and spiritual darkness can be attributed to the absence of divine light, and can be extinguished through the light of revealed scripture. Furthermore, the nature of light is such that it can be diminished using veils without diminishing the intensity of the original source of light in any way. The mystics write that similar is the light of scripture: It is powerfully intense and has the ability to illuminate, but there are veils of spiritual ailments (greed, jealousy, anger, and so on) in the soul that diminish the power of scriptural lights (41:5). As such, the mystics say that in order to gain illumination through scriptural teachings, a person must work on removing the veils that separate the heart from divine light.

8 For Qur'anic interpreters this is a criticism of some Jewish scholars who failed to live up to the responsibility of preserving scripture, and who looked to sources other than scripture to make ethical laws and judgments. In doing so, they basically sold the message of God for a trifling gain in this world. In this, there is a universal message for all: doctrines, values, and laws should conform to divine will, which is expressed in sacred scripture, rather than in the whims and desires of human beings.

9 In this passage there is a double emphasis on the idea that the core teachings and message of Jesus contained in the Gospel are in fact congruent with the values and ideals of the Torah. The original Gospel of Jesus was sent as a confirmation and reminder to the children of Israel, reflecting the same light and guidance found in the Torah. In the Islamic tradition, then, Jesus does not come to replace the law, but rather to fulfill it in accordance with divine will. Muslims believe that Jesus preached a Gospel that called on people to believe in One God and to willingly surrender to divine will, and that he never claimed to be God incarnate or the son of God (4:171–172).

It was We who revealed the Torah, in it guidance and light.[7] The prophets who surrendered to God judge the Jews thereby, as do the rabbis and the learned, for them was entrusted the protection of God's book, of which they were witnesses. Therefore be not in awe of men, but be in awe of Me, and sell not My signs for a petty price. And any who do fail to judge by what God has revealed are the ones who reject faith.[8]

—QUR'AN 5:44

And in their footsteps We sent Jesus the son of Mary, confirming the Torah that had come before him. We sent him the Gospel, therein guidance and light, and confirmation of Torah that had come before him, a guidance and admonition for those who are God-conscious. Then let the people of the Gospel judge by what God has revealed therein. If any do fail to judge by what God has revealed, it is they who are rebellious.[9]

—QUR'AN 5:46–47

10 For Muslims, this passage marks a vital understanding of revealed scripture: God's revelations are wholly and entirely consistent with one another, and the core doctrines and values always remain the same even if some of the specific wordings or laws differ to reflect the time and space of a particular revealed scripture. This is why we find such similarities between all world scriptures. More often differences are found in interpretation of scripture rather than in the actual teachings.

11 There is a conviction among Muslims that the Qur'an is divinely protected from corruption and change and preserved by God for all times to come. The Qur'an says about its own revelation, "Nay, this is a glorious recital, inscribed in a preserved tablet" (85:21–22). For some commentators the "preserved tablet" means there is literally a heavenly tablet that has preserved the book for all of eternity. Others take a more metaphorical understanding of the "preserved tablet" to mean that God has protected the Qur'an from any textual changes. Some mystical interpreters have said that the "preserved tablet" is actually a metaphor for the hearts of those who have memorized the entire Qur'an (*hufadzh*).

To you We sent the scripture in truth, confirming the scripture that came before it,[10] and preserving it.[11] So judge between them by what God has revealed, and follow not their vain desires, diverging from the truth that has come to you. To each among you have We prescribed a law, and a revealed way. If God had so willed, God would have made you a single people, but the plan is to test you in what God has given you. So strive as in a race in all virtues, the goal of you all is to God; it is God that will show you the truth of the matters in which you differ.

—QUR'AN 5:48

Happy are those who purify themselves, and glorify the name of their Guardian-Lord and pray. Nay, but you prefer the life of this world though the hereafter is better and more enduring. This is, indeed, in the earlier books, in the books of Abraham and Moses.

—QUR'AN 87:14–19

12 "Healing" is another way scripture has been described in the Qur'an, because the recital of the book is known to cure ailing souls. This is why beautiful and melodious recitation of the Qur'an is used especially at the bedside of a dying person to offer comfort and hope, or at a funeral to relieve the grief of mourners, or during any time of hardship and distress. The Qur'an says about its own recital, "For those who believe, their hearts find tranquility in the remembrance of God, for it is in the remembrance of God that hearts find tranquility" (13:28).

13 Revelation is also known as a "mercy" because Muslims believe that God could have simply left us to our own faculties in figuring out how to live in this world, but chose instead out of divine mercy to give clear guidance and instruction through scripture.

14 The word used here in Arabic is *dhzalimeen,* which carries many shades of meaning, including "unjust," "oppressor," and "wrong-doer." But perhaps the most fitting translation in this context is "evil-doer," because the word implies someone who is immersed in evil to the point that all his or her doings contain an element of evil.

15 In other words, those who constantly rebel against the path of God and immerse themselves in evil only drag themselves deeper and deeper into a state of loss, to the point that their spiritual faculties become blinded to the healing and merciful nature of scripture.

16 This passage represents a good summary of the Qur'anic purpose: to be a source of divine mercy and compassion to humanity, explaining all of God's teachings in a clear and succinct manner. In doing so, the Qur'an serves as a glad tiding to those who believe in One God and do righteous deeds; and as a warning to those who associate partners with God, are miserly in giving to the poor, and deny any sense of accountability in the afterlife.

And We reveal from the Qur'an that which is a healing[12] and a mercy[13] for those who believe. But for the evildoers[14] it causes nothing but loss.[15]

—QUR'AN 17:82

A revelation from the Merciful, the Compassionate—a book where the messages are explained in detail; a recital in Arabic for people of knowledge, to be a herald of good news as well as a warning, yet most of them turn away, and so they hear not. They say, "Our hearts are veiled from that to which you invite us to, and in our ears is deafness, and between us and you is a barrier; so do what you will, for we will do what we do." Say you [O Prophet], "I am but a mortal like you. It is revealed to me that your God is One God, so take the straight path to God and ask for forgiveness. And woe to those who join gods with God, and those who do not give alms, for it is they who deny the hereafter. As for those who believe and do good works, they shall have an unending reward."[16]

—QUR'AN 41:2–8

17 The Arabic word *muhkamat* has also been commonly translated as "precise," "basic," "fundamental," and "essential," the idea being that such verses have clear teachings, principles, and commandments to direct human life, as opposed to verses that use allegory and possess layers of meaning that are open to interpretation. Therefore *muhkamat* verses are foundational to the scripture.

18 The Arabic word *mutashabihat* can also be translated as "not entirely clear," "allegorical," and "vague." All of these translations probably do an injustice to the real meaning of the word, which comes from the word *shubha,* meaning "doubt." Another way *mutashabihat* can be defined is those verses that are expressed in a figurative manner with a meaning that is metaphorically implied but not directly stated. A good example of a *mutashabihat* verse on the nature of God is, "To God belong the east and the west, so wherever you turn, there is the Face of God, for God is omnipresent and omniscient" (2:115). Since Muslims do not believe in any form of anthropomorphism, we can conclude that the "Face of God" is an allegory for the "Presence of God" or "Essence of God," or something of that nature. As early Muslim theologians would put it, *bila kayf,* meaning "without how"—in other words, accepting that the "Face of God" (or any other ambiguous term) is real, but its precise meaning and nature is unknown.

19 Here the Qur'an warns against becoming obsessed, as some philosophers do, with the interpretation of ambiguous or allegorical verses to the point of ignoring the clear verses, which are really at the center of directing human beliefs and actions.

And this Qur'an is not something that could be manufactured without God; rather, it is a confirmation of what preceded it, and a fuller explanation of scripture, in which there is nothing dubious. That is from the Lord of all worlds. Do they say, "He forged it"? Say, "Then bring a chapter like it, and call upon anyone you can other than God, if you are being truthful."

—QUR'AN 10:37–38

These are the signs of the clearly expressed book. We have sent it down as an Arabic recital, in order that you may learn wisdom. We do relate unto you the most beautiful of stories, in that We reveal to you this Qur'an. Before this, you too were among those who knew it not.

—QUR'AN 12:1–3

It is God who has sent down to you the book, containing verses that are clear, which are the foundation of the book,[17] and others that are ambiguous.[18] As for those in whose hearts is perversity, they follow the ambiguous part, seeking discord, and searching for its final meaning ...[19]

—QUR'AN 3:7

(continued on page 35)

20 The majority of Qur'anic interpreters recite this passage with a pause after "but no one knows its complete meanings except God" in order to separate it from "And those deeply rooted in knowledge." However, there is a difference of opinion on the matter, and a good number of Qur'anic interpreters argue that the pause in recitation should come after "And those deeply rooted in knowledge." In other words, they would read the passage as "but no one knows its complete meanings except God and those deeply rooted in knowledge." If we read the passage according to the first opinion, it means that no one has access to the real meaning of allegorical verses except God; but if we recite this passage according to the second opinion, it means that God and those deeply rooted in knowledge have access to the mysteries of ambiguous verses. Sufis and Shias tend to recite this passage in the latter style because a core part of their doctrine says that there are men and women (*waliee 'Allah* or "friends of God" for Sufis; *ayat 'Allah* or "sign of God" for Shias) who reach a level of insight and wisdom into the scripture that allows them to discover the hidden meanings of *mutashabihat* verses. These differing takes on the passage also have a strong implication on the question of who has authority in the tradition and where that authority comes from. For the former school of thought authority lies with the scholars, but such authority exists only to the extent that the scholar is able to make a convincing argument with definite proofs. For the latter school of thought, *walee 'Allah* or *ayat 'Allah* carry greater authority in interpreting divine will, because they possess unique insight and understanding of scripture.

… but no one knows its complete meanings except God.[20] And those deeply rooted in knowledge say, "We believe in it, the whole of it is from our Sustainer." And none will grasp this except those with deep understanding.

—QUR'AN 3:7

The one who was devoted to the recitation of the Qur'an will be told on the Day of Resurrection, "Go on reciting and ascending in ranks as carefully and distinctly as you used to recite carefully and distinctly when you were in the world. Your station will be at the last verse of your recitation."

—PROPHET MUHAMMAD

Any group of people that assemble in one of the Houses of God in order to recite the book of God and to teach it to one another, tranquility will descend upon them, mercy will cover them, angels will spread their wings over them and God will make mention of them to those around.

—PROPHET MUHAMMAD

21 The Night of Power, known as *laylat al-qadr,* is the actual day on which the Qur'an was first revealed to Prophet Muhammad. As such, it is considered a specially blessed night in the month of Ramadan in which every act of worship or good deed is multiplied in reward as if it were done over a period of a thousand months. It is a night filled with divine mercy and forgiveness for anyone who actively seeks it, and is also a night in which every soul's destiny is decided for the year to come, similar to the ten days between Rosh Hashanah and Yom Kippur in the Jewish tradition. Interestingly, the Night of Power is not really known, but most Muslims believe it is anytime during the last ten nights of Ramadan, while others believe that it is one of the odd nights during the last ten nights of Ramadan.

22 This verse was revealed first and foremost to Prophet Muhammad, but its lesson is applicable to all: Do not become impatient with the learning or mastery of the Qur'an, for complete understanding can only be gained with patience and time.

23 Here again Prophet Muhammad is gently reminded by God not to be impatient with the recitation of the Qur'an, and in so doing there is a lesson for all students of the Qur'an: scripture is not meant to be recited quickly or hastily, but rather slowly with deep reflection and contemplation. If this method is employed in studying the Qur'an, then God will make clear its manifest teachings and inner wisdoms.

We have indeed revealed this [scripture] on the Night of Power. And what will make you understand what the Night of Power is? The Night of Power is better than a thousand months. Therein come down the angels and the spirit by God's permission, on every affair. Peace, till the rise of dawn.[21]

—QUR'AN 97

Exalted is God, the true king! Be not in haste with the Qur'an before its revelation to you is completed, but say, "O my Sustainer, increase me in knowledge."[22]

—QUR'AN 20:114

Do not hasten your tongue about this [revelation] to hurry with it, for its collection and its recital are up to Us, so when We have recited it, then follow its recital, for its explanation is up to Us.[23]

—QUR'AN 75:16–19

The best amongst you is the one who learns the Qur'an and teaches it.

—PROPHET MUHAMMAD

He who has nothing of the Qur'an in his heart is like a ruined house.

—PROPHET MUHAMMAD

[1] Prophetic stories in the Qur'an, some of which are mentioned in this chapter, are not meant merely for storytelling or legend making, but rather for the important goals of moral instruction and spiritual guidance. The ones most likely to benefit from these stories are those who reflect deeply within themselves on the moral of the narrative and how it relates to human life.

[2] The very purpose of prophets and messengers on earth is to deliver the divine message, which is that moral, ethical, and good behavior will see its good fruits in both this world and the hereafter; and immoral, unethical, and reprehensible behavior will see its evil fruits in this life and the hereafter. So, those who follow the prophetic way attain to a state of happiness and tranquility that removes fear and grief from their hearts.

[3] Prophets and messengers are sent to articulate and clarify the divine message that is contained in revealed scripture. The role of these prophets is simply to convey the teachings; the attainment of guidance is between human beings and God.

[4] The divine message carried by prophets and messengers to humanity was sent, according to Qur'anic teachings, to every place on earth so that the knowledge of good and evil would be made well known to all communities. As a result, some people in every prophetic community took to guidance and others rejected it. We are told to travel and study the nature of those nations that went against divine teachings and principles and in doing so caused their own demise. Many famous Muslim historians, such as Ibn Battuta, place this verse at the beginning of their books to show that a study of history is in fact a divinely enjoined science.

4 □ On Prophetic Character and Message

There is in their stories instruction for men endued with understanding. It is not a tale invented, but a confirmation of what went before it, a detailed exposition of all things, and a guide and a mercy to any who believe.[1]

—QUR'AN 12:111

We send the Messengers only to give good news and to warn, so those who believe and mend their ways have nothing to fear, and they will not sorrow.[2]

—QUR'AN 6:48

We sent not a messenger except to teach in the language of his own people in order to bring them clarity of understanding. And God allows people to stray at will, and guides any at will, and God is exalted in power, full of wisdom.[3]

—QUR'AN 14:4

For We assuredly sent amongst every people a Messenger, telling them to serve God, and abstain from evil. Of the people were some whom God guided, and some who inevitably went astray. So travel through the earth and see what the end was of those who rejected the truth.[4]

—QUR'AN 16:36

5 As honored as the prophets and messengers are, the Qur'an reminds us that in the end they are human beings who lived and died, and can therefore never be equal to God or somehow be worshiped in place of the divine. This is why the Qur'an also says specifically to the Muslims, "Muhammad is no more than a messenger. Many were the messengers that passed away before him. If he died or were slain, will you then turn back on your heels? If any did turn back on his heels, not the least harm will he do to God; but God will quickly reward those who are grateful" (3:144). When Prophet Muhammad did pass away, his best friend and the community's new leader, Abu Bakr, said, "If any of you worshiped Muhammad, know that he has died; but if you worship God, know that God is alive and will never die."

6 One of the many arguments levied against Prophet Muhammad by those who rejected his message was that if God truly wanted to send a sign, then why would it be in the form of a man like themselves and not in the form of a more heavenly creature, like an angel (Qur'an 25:7–9). The Qur'anic response to this question is that God sends messengers in the form of human beings so that humanity will have an excellent example of how best to serve and worship God. Had God sent angels to deliver the message, human beings would have said that there is no way to replicate the actions and character of an angelic being.

Before you, also the messengers We sent were but human beings to whom We granted inspiration. If you know this not, ask of those who possess the message. Nor did We give them bodies that ate no food, nor were they immortals.[5]

—QUR'AN 21:7–8

What kept men back from belief when guidance came to them was nothing but this: they said, "Has God sent a man like us to be a messenger?" Say, "If there were settled on earth angels walking about in peace and quiet, We should certainly have sent them down from the heavens an angel for a messenger."[6]

—QUR'AN 17:94–95

Their messenger said: "Is there a doubt about God, the Creator of the heavens and the earth? It is God who invites you, in order that God may forgive you your sins and give you respite for a term appointed!" They said: "Ah, You are no more than human, like us. You wish to turn us away from what our fathers used to worship, so then bring us some clear authority." Their messengers said to them: "True, we are human like you, but God does grant divine grace to such servants as God pleases. It is not for us to bring you an authority except as God permits, and on God let all people of faith put their trust. We have no reason not to trust God since God has guided us in our ways. We shall certainly bear with patience all the hurt you may cause us. And let the trusting put their trust in God."

—QUR'AN 14:10–12

7 | The Qur'an finds its theological roots in the teachings and creed of Abraham, who is known as the "father of faith." It is for this reason that Muslims consider themselves to be under the rubric of the Abrahamic faiths, along with Judaism and Christianity. Interestingly, in this passage Abraham's creed is described as *islam* and he himself is called a *muslim*. This is because the linguistic meaning of *islam* is "surrender to the will of God," and the linguistic meaning of *muslim* is "one who has surrendered to the will of God." With this definition in mind, the Qur'an makes the argument that Abraham was indeed someone who always surrendered his will to God, and therefore his religion was the path of *islam*, and he characterized the essence of what it means to be *muslim*. After Abraham, Jacob and his sons are also portrayed as those who surrender to the will of God, *muslim*. As such, we can conclude that the Qur'anic teaching here is that at the core of every prophetic message is a call for people to surrender themselves to the will of God (*islam*). Muslims do not see Islam as a new religion that Prophet Muhammad brought into existence, but rather as the religion of all the prophets since the beginning of time, culminating in the final teachings of Prophet Muhammad.

8 | According to the Qur'an, Muslims must believe in all of the prophets who came before Muhammad, including those mentioned in the Hebrew Bible and the Christian New Testament. Abraham is the father of faith in that he fathered Ishmael, from whose lineage the great Arab prophets came, including Muhammad; and he fathered Isaac, from whose lineage the great Hebrew prophets emanated, including Moses and Jesus.

And who turns away from the creed of Abraham but those who make fools of themselves? Him We chose and rendered pure in this world and he will be in the hereafter in the ranks of the righteous. When his Sustainer said to him, "Surrender yourself to Me," he answered, "I have surrendered myself to the Sustainer of all the worlds."[7] And Abraham enjoined upon his sons as did Jacob: "O my sons! God has chosen the faith for you, so die not except in a state of surrender to the will of God. Were you witnesses when death appeared before Jacob? Behold, he said to his sons: "What will you worship after me?" They answered, "We shall worship your God and that of your fathers, of Abraham, Ishmael, and Isaac—the One God, to whom we surrender ourselves."[8]

—QUR'AN 2:130–133

Say, "We believe in God, and the revelation given to us, and to Abraham, Ishmael, Isaac, Jacob, and the Tribes, and that given to Moses and Jesus, and that given to all prophets from their Guardian-Lord. We make no difference between one and another of them, and we surrender ourselves to God."

—QUR'AN 2:136

✦ There are some twenty-five prophets mentioned by name in the Qur'an. Some of their stories, such as those of Abraham and Moses, are told quite extensively and mentioned throughout the scripture. Other prophets are mentioned only once or twice in the entire book. However, the Qur'an is clear that there were many other prophets and messengers who came throughout time but who are not mentioned in the scripture: "We did aforetime send messengers before you. Of them there are some whose story We have related to you, and some whose story We have not related to you...." (40:78). In this chapter I focus only on a few prophetic stories to give you a taste of the Qur'anic narrative on them.

9 This passage is a summary of Prophet Noah's story, which is mentioned several times and in more detail in other parts of the Qur'an. The portrait of Noah is that of a man who patiently preached the message of God to his people for 950 years until God sent a flood to destroy all those who persisted in sin and evil while saving Noah and his followers in the ark. Here Noah, like Abraham, is described as *muslim*—someone who surrendered to the will of God. Noah is regarded in Islamic theology as one of the five greatest prophets. In another passage Noah offers a supplication for safe traveling before embarking on the ark that is recited by Muslims to this day every time they begin a journey: "Let its [the means of transportation] course and its mooring proceed by the name of God" (11:41). The moral of Noah's story is that no matter how much time a person spends on earth calling people to righteous conduct, there will always be many who reject this counsel for more worldly gains. Such people will experience their own demise, whereas those who patiently persevere in belief and goodness will be protected and brought to the safe shores of divine presence.

Relate to them the story of Noah. Behold, he said to his people, "O my people, if my presence and my recollection of the signs of God are a hardship on you, I put my trust in God. So gather an agreement about your plan and among your partners, so your plan be not to you dark and dubious. Then pass your sentence on me, and give me no respite. But if you turn back, know that no reward have I asked of you. My reward is only due from God, and I have been commanded to be of those who surrender to God's will." They rejected him, but We delivered him, and those with him, in the ark, and We made them inherit the earth while We drowned in the flood those who rejected Our signs. Then see what the end was of those who were warned [but heeded not].[9]

—QUR'AN 10:71–72

And God taught Adam all names, then set them forth to the angels and said, "Tell Me these names, if you are truthful." They said, "Glory to You! We have no knowledge but what you have taught us. It is You who are the Knowing, the Wise." God said, "Adam, tell them the names." And when he had told them the names, God said, "Did I not say to you that I know the secrets of the heavens and the earth? And I know what you reveal and what you have been hiding."

—QUR'AN 2:31–33

10 This passage confirms Prophet Abraham's status as the leader of the faithful and an example of excellence in devotion to God. Abraham's story is found throughout the Qur'an, and much of it is a confirmation of what we find in the biblical account of Genesis. This particular story, however, is found only in the Qur'an and gives us some sense of the origins of Islam. Abraham is shown building the House of God with his son Ishmael for the sole purpose of worshiping and glorifying the divine. This House of God is known as the *kabba* located in the ancient city of Mecca, and Muslims visit this sanctuary from all around the world throughout the year, particularly during the annual pilgrimage known as the Hajj, which in part commemorates the life, struggles, sacrifices, and achievements of Abraham, Hagar, and their son Ishmael. So, the Qur'an here fills out the untold story found in Genesis, which leaves the story of Ishmael and Hagar hanging with no conclusive end. In this story, Muslims find their historical roots in the religion of Abraham and his son Ishmael, from whose lineage Prophet Muhammad is born many generations later.

11 For Muslims, Prophet Muhammad is God's answer to the supplication of Abraham and Ishmael for a city of peace, a community that surrenders to the will of God, and a messenger who brings guidance and wisdom.

12 Ishmael—the first son born to Abraham—is given an honorable description in part as a refutation to the less than flattering description we find of him in Genesis 16. Ishmael, like his father and brother Isaac, was a righteous prophet and messenger who encouraged spiritual devotion and charity among his people. In his footsteps came Prophet Muhammad, who restored the same values and principles to the land of Mecca.

And remember that Abraham was tried by his Guardian-Lord with certain commands, which he fulfilled, then God said, "I will make you a leader to humanity. Abraham pleaded, "And also from my offspring!" God answered, "But My promise is not within reach of evildoers." Remember We made the House a place of assembly for humanity and a place of safety; and take you the station of Abraham as a place of prayer, for We commanded Abraham and Ishmael that they should sanctify My House for those who will walk around it, or use it as a retreat, or bow, or prostrate themselves in prayer.[10] And remember Abraham said, "My Guardian-Lord, make this a city of peace, and feed its people with fruits, such as them as believe in God and the last day" ... And remember Abraham and Ishmael raised the foundations of the House [and they prayed]: "Our Sustainer, accept this service from us, for You are the All-Hearing, the All-Knowing. Our Sustainer, make us among those surrendering to You and of our progeny a people who surrender themselves to You, and show us our place for the celebration of due rites, and turn to us, for You are the Acceptor of Repentance, the Merciful. Our Sustainer, send amongst them a messenger of their own, who shall rehearse Your signs to them and instruct them in scripture and wisdom, and purify them, for You are the Almighty, the Wise."[11]

—QUR'AN 2:124–129

Also mention in the book Ishmael, for he was true to what he promised, and he was a messenger and a prophet. He used to enjoin on his people prayer and almsgiving and he was most acceptable in the sight of his Guardian-Lord.[12]

—QUR'AN 19:55–56

13 Some biblical scholars have claimed that the present-day conflict between Jews and Muslims was born out of an ancient rivalry, as depicted in Genesis, between Isaac and Ishmael. However, this is an unacceptable notion for Muslims, because both Ishmael and Isaac are honored in the Qur'an as noble and righteous prophets of God who brought the same divine teachings and values to two separate lands for future generations. Ishmael and Isaac were not hostile rivals, but rather friendly brothers to each other. Thus, any hostility between the descendants of Ishmael and Isaac is not natural as some would claim. What is natural and befitting, according to the Qur'anic narrative, is friendship and brotherhood between the descendants of two great prophets.

14 This passage concludes the story of Joseph, the only story in the Qur'an that is relayed from beginning to end in one chapter. Joseph's story is a celebration of the fact that God's plan is always greater than the plan of those who spread mischief on earth, and it is a celebration of the power of forgiveness that Joseph exhibits toward his brothers despite their evil plot against him. In this particular passage we find Joseph thanking his Sustainer for giving him the gift of dream interpretation, which won him freedom from prison and a high position in Pharaoh's court. Like prophets before him, Joseph surrenders his will to God. The story of Joseph is described as the most beautiful of stories in the Qur'an (12:3) because it teaches us that if we believe in God and act according to divine instruction, we will always prevail in the end, even if we experience temporary hardship. Prophet Joseph also teaches us one of the most important lessons of life: it is always better and more righteous to forgive, even those who may have done the worst of things to us, because in doing so we free our own souls from the anger and hatred that result from holding grudges against people.

And We bestowed on [Abraham] Isaac and, as an additional gift Jacob, and We made righteous men of them all. And We made them leaders, guiding by our command, and We inspired them to do good deeds, to establish regular prayers, to give alms, and they constantly served Us.[13]

—Qur'an 21:72–73

[Joseph said]: "O my Sustainer! You have indeed bestowed on me some power, and taught me something of the interpretation of dreams, O creator of the heavens and the earth. You are my protector in this world and in the hereafter. Take You, then, my soul as one who has surrendered to Your will, and unite me with the righteous."[14]

—Qur'an 12:101

And remember Our servant Job, for behold he cried to his Sustainer, "Satan has afflicted me with distress and suffering!" [God said]: "Strike the earth with your foot, here is water wherein to wash, cool, and a refreshing drink." And We gave him back his people and doubled their number as a mercy from Us, and a thing for remembrance for all those who possess deep understanding. "And take in your hand a little grass, and strike with it and break not your oath." Truly We found him full of patience, an excellent servant; for he constantly turned to God.

—Qur'an 38:41–44

15 The prophetic experience of Moses is the most mentioned story in the Qur'an. In many ways, Prophet Muhammad's life is very similar to the life of Prophet Moses—both were sent to liberate the poor and weak from an oppressive political system, both challenged the system and were in turn persecuted, both were forced to flee to another land where they became leaders of an entire nation and were made to play the dual roles of spiritual healers and political reformers, and both were eventually successful in giving victory to their people. For this reason, the prophetic example and character of Moses is often revealed in the Qur'an to strengthen Prophet Muhammad's resolve and to remind him of the fruits of faith and patience. For us, too, there are moral lessons in the modern world. First, in order to be successful in changing an oppressive sociopolitical order, we must possess enormous strength of character, nobility, and wisdom, such as that of Prophet Moses. Second, resisting and seeking to change a tyrannical sociopolitical order is a noble undertaking and one that is aided by the power of God. Third, when we are delivered from sociopolitical oppression, we must show gratitude to God by working for a more just and peaceful order in the world, rather than becoming the very oppressors from whom we once fled.

16 This passage is revealed in praise of Prophet David, who developed both external and internal power to become one of history's most celebrated figures. David is given the strength to defeat Goliath (Qur'an, 2:251), the illumination to be in constant devotion to God with the rest of nature, and the wisdom to judge justly between people (Qur'an, 38:21–26). The character of Prophet David represents the enormous human capacity to be a revolutionary, a spiritual sage, and a just leader all at once, if those abilities are developed in a wholesome manner. This speaks to the worldview of Islam, which does not divide spirituality and law into different categories, but rather combines them as complementary elements of human life and society. Prophet Solomon's story reflects this in a very similar manner as well (Qur'an 27:15–19).

We also blessed Moses and Aaron, and We rescued them and their people from tremendous trouble, and We helped them so they would be victors, and We gave them the clear scripture, and We guided them to the straight path, and We left for them [followers] in future generations. "Peace upon Moses and Aaron!" For that is how We recompense those who do good; for those two were among Our faithful servants.[15]

—QUR'AN 37:114–122

Have patience at what they say, and remember Our servant David, the man of strength, for he constantly returned to God. It was We that made the hills declare, in unison with him, Our praises in the evening and at sunrise. And the birds gathered all with him to turn to God. We strengthened his kingdom, and gave him wisdom and sound judgment in speech and decision.[16]

—QUR'AN 38:17–20

17 The story of Jesus is mentioned in several places in the Qur'an, for he is one of the most honored and respected messengers in the eyes of Muslims. Jesus is said to have been born of virgin birth to Mary and sent as a messenger specifically to the children of Israel with special miraculous signs and consistent prophetic teachings. While Muslims and Christians both revere Jesus, there are some key beliefs about his life and teachings that differ between the two traditions. The Qur'an says that the plot of the enemies of Jesus to crucify him did not actually work and in reality God raised Jesus up to the heavens without his experiencing crucifixion or death (4:157–158). The Qur'an says that Jesus was a righteous prophet and messenger of God who called himself a servant of God and called people to the worship and service of One God (4:172, 5:17, 9:30–31). The Qur'an does not claim that he was God incarnate or the son of God.

18 Prophet Muhammad was given the same role as the messengers that came before him, namely to serve as a guide out of the depths of spiritual darkness and into the light of spiritual illumination through sincere counsel. The Prophet, like prophets before him, faced many enemies who sought to extinguish the light of his teachings. The scripture tells him to ignore and overlook the enemy's taunts while holding fast to divine trust. In this is a lesson for us too: the taunts and opposition we may face in the path of goodness should not distract us from righteous works. The key to patience in the face of immoral opposition is to trust and rely on God.

[Jesus was] a messenger to the children of Israel: "I have come to you, with a sign from your Sustainer, in that I make for you out of clay, as it were, the figure of a bird, and breathe into it, and it becomes a bird by divine permission; and I heal the blind and the leprous, and I bring the dead back to life by divine permission; and I tell you what you eat, and what you store in your houses. Surely therein is a sign for you if you are believers. And attesting to the Torah before me, and to make permissible to you part of what was forbidden to you; I have come to you with a sign from your Sustainer. So be conscious of God, and obey me. It is God who is my Sustainer and your Sustainer; then worship God. This is a way that is straight. When Jesus found unbelief on their part he said, "Who will be my helpers on the way to God? Said the disciples, "We are God's helpers for we believe in God; witness, then, that we surrender ourselves to the will of God: "Our Sustainer, we believe in what you have revealed and we follow the messenger, then write us down among those who bear witness. Yet they plotted [against Jesus] but God plotted too, for God is the best of planners."[17]

—QUR'AN 3:49–54

O Prophet, truly We have sent you as a witness, a bearer of glad tidings and a warner, and as one who invites to God by divine permission, and as an illuminating lamp. Then give the glad tidings to the believers that they shall have from God a very great reward. And follow not the rejecters of faith and the hypocrites, and ignore their insults; and trust in God, for God is enough as a patron.[18]

—QUR'AN 33:45–48

19 Prophet Muhammad is presented as the ideal role model for a righteous, ethical, and moral life on earth as God's servant and devotee. Prophet Muhammad is mentioned very few times by name in the Qur'an, but it can be argued that in every passage of the Qur'an we can find the Prophet's shadow in the form of his teachings, debates, trials, victories, or spiritual experiences.

20 The chief characteristic of Prophet Muhammad was mercy, just as the chief attribute of God is Mercy. Throughout his life, the Prophet was verbally and physically abused by those who rejected his message, yet his response to them was always patience and forgiveness. In one episode of the Prophet's life he went to the city of Taif near Mecca where the people abused him till blood poured from his sandals. After the Prophet took safe refuge under a tree, the angel Gabriel came to him and said that he could bring the two mountains of Taif together to crush the city and its inhabitants for what they had done to him. But the Prophet refused, saying that he hoped future generations from this city would worship and serve God with devotion. He then prayed for the people's forgiveness by saying, "O God, forgive them for they do not know." It is after this incident that God gave Prophet Muhammad the title of "mercy for all creatures." If we are to follow in the footsteps of this noble messenger, then our words, deeds, and conduct should be characterized by prophet-like mercy and kindness.

You have indeed in the messenger of God an excellent example for the one who longs for God and the last day, and remembers God abundantly.[19]

—QUR'AN 33:21

We sent you not, except as a mercy for all creatures.[20]

—QUR'AN 21:107

It is part of the Mercy of God that you do deal gently with them. Were you severe or harsh-hearted, they would have broken away from you; so pass over [their faults], and ask for forgiveness for them; and consult them in affairs. Then, when you have taken a decision put your trust in God, for God loves the trusting.

—QUR'AN 3:159

By the Qur'an, full of Wisdom, you are indeed one of the messengers, on a straight way. It is a revelation sent down by the Exalted in Might, the Merciful, in order that thou may admonish a people whose fathers had received no admonition, and who therefore remain heedless.

—QUR'AN 36:2–6

1 The Arabic term *ya'budoon* comes from *'ibada,* meaning "worship," which comes from the root word *'abd,* meaning "servant" or "devotee." As such, *ya'budoon* has often been translated as either "worship" or "serve," but I feel that a linguistic study of the word encompasses both definitions. Hence, I have given the term *ya'budoon* a more comprehensive translation of "worship and serve."

2 For Muslims, the very purpose of human life is to worship and serve the divine by surrendering themselves to God. Becoming a servant of God does not only entail prescribed prayers or invocations, but in reality demands that we commit to a way of living, speaking, and walking that is in sync with divine teachings. At the core of worship and service to God is practicing generosity, kindness, and compassion toward God's creation. In the end, we worship and serve God for the benefit of our own souls and to fulfill the purpose of our creation; for God's dominion neither increases nor decreases with our behavior.

3 The idea of surrendering to the will of God is natural and instinctual in a pure heart, according to the Qur'an. When a man once came to visit Prophet Muhammad and the Prophet asked, "Have you come to ask about righteousness?" The man replied, "Yes, O messenger of God." The Prophet replied, "Consult your own heart." In other words, the pure heart naturally possesses the ability to distinguish between truth and falsehood, good and evil, and thus the purpose of life becomes natural if we remain true to the calling of our conscience. In other words, the purpose of life need not be taught, but only discovered within our own hearts.

5 □ On the Purpose and Responsibility of Human Life

And I have not created invisible spirits and human beings, except that they may worship and serve Me.[1] No sustenance do I require of them, nor do I require that they should feed Me, for it is God who gives sustenance, the Lord of all might, forever strong.[2]

—QUR'AN 51:56–58

So set your face to the religion as God-given nature, according to which God created humanity, for there is no altering the creation of God— that is the true religion, but most among humankind know not.[3]

—QUR'AN 30:30

Say: "Is it someone other than God that you order me to worship, O you ignorant ones?" But it has already been revealed to you, as it was to those before you, "If you were to join [gods with God], truly fruitless will be your work [in life], and you will surely be in the ranks of those who lose." Nay, but worship God, and be of those who give thanks.

—QUR'AN 39:64–66

Whoever submits his whole self to God, and is a beautifully excellent devotee, has grasped indeed the most trustworthy handhold. And with God rests the end and decision of every affair.

—QUR'AN 31:22

4 The role given to human beings on earth is to be representatives or deputies of God on earth. The very act of representing entails a close adherence to the will of the one being represented and an embodiment of the qualities and values of that which is represented. For example, a good ambassador of any nation will act and speak only in a way that is in harmony with the will of his or her nation, and in doing so will epitomize the nation's qualities and values. Similarly, a noble representative or deputy of God will speak and act only in ways that have been made permissible by the divine, and will try to best reflect the beautiful attributes of God in his or her actions and behavior.

5 All human beings are given special gifts, abilities, circumstances, and social positions in life as a test to see how well they fulfill their role as representatives of God on earth. A rich person, for example, is tested in his or her generosity and sense of giving; a poor person in his or her patience and sense of gratitude. In the end, the rich who pass their test move closer to God's attribute as the Generous (al-kareem), and the poor who pass their test come closer to God's attribute as the Patient (al-sabur) and the Grateful (al-shakur). In doing so, both the rich and the poor experience something of divine nature and are then in a better position to be noble deputies of God on earth.

6 Being a deputy of God on earth is no reason to be haughty or abusive, but rather the position of deputy is one of responsibility and requires a humble attitude toward all of God's creation.

7 Righteousness is not found in mere rituals or motions that are devoid of belief and pious conduct. This is an essential point of understanding for the believer since worshiping and serving God, the purpose of life itself, can become ritualistic if it is done without proper intention, meaning, and spirit. So the essence of worship requires a deep sense of devotion to God, a desire to assist all fellow human beings whether they are related or complete strangers, and patience and gratitude to God in all circumstances. It is only then that we truly and consciously fulfill our life's purpose and our role as deputies of God on earth.

It is God who has made you deputies on the earth,[4] raising you in ranks, some above others, in order to test you in the gifts God gave you.[5] Verily, your Guardian-Lord is swift in retribution, yet is truly forgiving and merciful.[6]

—QUR'AN 6:165

It is not [the mark of] righteousness that you turn your faces toward east or west. Rather, truly righteous are those who believe in God and the last day, and the angels and the scriptures, and the prophets; and who give material gifts out of love for God, even of what they care for, to relatives and orphans, and the poor and the traveler and the needy, and for the freeing of slaves; and who establish prayer and give alms; and who fulfill their promises which they have made; and those who are patient in misfortune, affliction, and hardship—such are the people of truth, and they are the God-conscious ones.[7]

—QUR'AN 2:177

8 The gift of human faculties is given to us as part of our responsibility to fulfill our purpose and role on earth. As such, every aspect of human faculty must be used for the higher purpose of worshiping the divine rather than satisfying our own lower desires or pleasures.

9 Qur'anic commentators have understood "the two highways" to mean the paths of good and evil, both of which are expounded upon in great detail in the scripture.

10 Once again we see an emphasis on action that is rooted in showing generosity and compassion toward fellow human beings. For the devout Muslim, then, sitting idly at home while the world is in despair is not a genuine option. The path of good has been described as "the steep uphill road" because by its nature it requires struggle and hard work. Meanwhile the path of evil is easy since it simply requires basking in the glory of lower desires. In the end, if you commit yourself to being a servant of God who climbs "the steep uphill road," you will get to experience the beauty of the mountain top; but if you choose the easy downward path, you will eventually hit rock bottom.

11 "Companions of the right hand" is a term used in the Qur'an to describe those who will be in a happy state on the day of accountability because they will have earned divine mercy and forgiveness, having at least tried to fulfill the purpose of life and their role on earth.

Have We not made [for human beings] two eyes, and a tongue, and two lips?**8** And shown him the two highways?**9** But he has not braved the steep uphill road. And what will explain to you what the steep uphill road is? [It is] freeing the slave, or the giving of food on a day of hunger to the orphaned relative or a needy stranger lying in the dust. Then will he be of those who believe, and enjoin patience and enjoin compassion.**10** Such are the companions of the right hand.**11**

—Qur'an 90:8–18

"O son of Adam, I fell ill and you visited Me not." He will say: "O Guardian-Lord, and how should I visit You when You are the Lord of the worlds?" God will say: "Did you not know that My servant so-and-so had fallen ill and you visited him not? Did you not know that had you visited him you would have found Me with him?" [Then God will say]: "O son of Adam, I asked you for food and you fed Me not." He will say: "O Guardian-Lord, and how should I feed You when You are the Lord of the worlds?" God will say: "Did you not know that My servant so-and-so asked you for food and you fed him not? Did you not know that had you fed him you would surely have found Me with him?" [Then God will say]: "O son of Adam, I asked you to give Me to drink and you gave Me not to drink." He will say: "O Lord, how should I give You to drink when You are the Lord of the worlds?" God will say: "My servant so-and-so asked you for drink, and you gave him not to drink. Had you given him to drink you would have surely found Me with him."

—Divine saying related by Prophet Muhammad

1 In Islamic theology, the human experience of every one of us began even before we were conceived and born into earthly life. Our story began with a primordial event in which God gathered all the souls of humanity to testify about the truthfulness and Oneness of God as Lord and Sustainer, and we in turn collectively bore witness to this reality. It is believed by Muslims, then, that all human beings possess innate knowledge of God in their hearts and are naturally inclined to worship and surrender themselves to divine will as a result of this pre-earthly covenant between God and humanity. In Islamic rituals a new-born baby is immediately reminded of this covenant when the call to prayer (known as the *adhzan* in Arabic) is recited into his or her right ear. Therefore, it is believed that every human being is born in a state of complete innocence and purity, rather than in a state of "original sin." For this reason Muslims also believe that any child who dies before the age of maturity is admitted directly into paradise to reside in the beautiful house of Prophet Abraham.

✦ Magians were priests in religious settlements from Mesopotamia and the surrounding region, and existed up until the Christian epoch. They believed in the old nature religion of Iran, which preceded Zoroastrianism. The most famous Magians were the "Wise Men from the East" who, according to the Gospel of Matthew, journeyed to Bethlehem bearing gifts for the young Jesus.

6 □ On the Stages of Human Life

When your Lord drew forth from the Children of Adam—from their loins—their descendants, and made them testify concerning themselves, [saying]: "Am I not your Lord?" They said, "Yes indeed, we do testify!"[1]

—QUR'AN 7:172

Every newborn is born into a state of natural inclination [to worship One God], and it is his parents who make him into a Jew, Christian, or Magian.

—PROPHET MUHAMMAD

2 This *hadith* elucidates further the sophisticated and careful design of God in its several different stages. The common scientific and moral question of when life begins is answered in Islamic theology through this prophetic saying, which indicates that the angel Gabriel blows the spirit of life into the fetus after 120 days.

3 In Islamic theology it is believed that God has predestined certain aspects of our lives while we are still in the wombs of our mothers, such as the source and amount of wealth we acquire, the time and place of our death, the choices we are presented with that determine our actions, and whether our lives are filled with fortune or misfortune. Muslims constantly acknowledge divine destiny by invoking terms such as "If God wills" (*Insha'Allah*) when referring to the future, "With the will of God" (*Masha'Allah*) to indicate an acceptance of divine decree, "Glory be to God" (*Subhana'Allah*) when expressing joy or astonishment at God's Will, and "There is no power except through God" (*la hawla walaa quwata illa billah*) as a means of protection against evil and a reminder of reality.

4 It is important to understand, though, that within the realm of actions, God predestines your choices and even creates the capability for you to act (Qur'an 37:96), but ultimately it is you who acquire a choice from among the choices God presents, and it is you who perform the act that God has made you capable of performing, and therefore it is you who bear the moral responsibility for any good or evil that you do (Qur'an 15:92–93).

5 Everything that was, is, and will be is part of God's pre-eternal Knowledge, and this includes the final destiny in the hereafter for each of us.

Verily the creation of each one of you is brought together in his mother's belly for forty days in the form of seed, then he is a clot of blood for a like period, then a morsel of flesh for a like period, then there is sent to him the angel who blows the breath of life into him[2] and who is commanded about four matters:[3] to write down his means of livelihood, his life span, his actions,[4] and whether happy or unhappy. By God, other than Whom there is no god, verily one of you behaves like the people of Paradise until there is but an arm's length between him and it, and that which has been written over takes him and so he behaves like the people of hellfire and thus he enters it; and one of you behaves like the people of hellfire until there is but an arm's length between him and it, and that which has been written overtakes him and so he behaves like the people of Paradise and thus he enters it.[5]

—PROPHET MUHAMMAD

6 Here the Qur'an elucidates for us the sophisticated and intricate manner in which we were created by God as a reminder of God's creative powers that will be used to resurrect us from the graves long after our earthly passing. It is also a reminder of our humble origins as human beings, lest we become arrogant and think of ourselves as self-sufficient. A common saying in the Islamic tradition is, "From humble origins we come, and to humble origins are we to return." Interestingly, the Qur'an offers a parallel between human life and vegetation: Just as there are seasons in which vegetative lands go through birth, development, maturity, decline, death, and rebirth, we, too, go through all these different stages in our lives. And just as vegetation needs particular care during the birth and development, we, too, need extra attention during our youth to gain proper physical, intellectual, and spiritual maturity. Just as the vegetation peaks in its grandeur and usefulness in maturity, we, too, are expected to use the strength of our maturity for doing good works and producing benefit in the world. Then, just as the vegetation experiences a stage of decline and eventually death, we, too, experience a period of weakness and limitation that prepares us for an inevitable death. Lastly, just as the vegetative lands are renewed every year through the blessing of rain, we, too, are resurrected and brought before God on the Day of Accountability. Understanding these human stages of life allows us to prioritize our roles and responsibilities during each season of life we experience on earth.

7 Human beings are endowed with the most functional bodies, sophisticated intellects, and greatest potential for reaching spiritual proximity with God (17:70) so that we can function in the role of caretakers and stewards on earth as deputies of God. When we abandon this trust by indulging in evil instead of good on earth, we go from being the "best of molds" to the "lowest of the low" (Qur'an 7:179). However, the Qur'an offers a way out of this condition by advising us to believe, trust in, and be conscious of God in our minds, with our tongues, in our hearts, and through our limbs, by engaging in good and virtuous deeds that are a natural manifestation of sincere belief.

O humanity, if you are in doubt about the resurrection, remember that We created you from dust, then from a drop, then from a clot, then from a lump of flesh, formed and unformed, in order to edify you. And We keep in the womb those who We wish, up to a designated term; then We bring you out as infants, and enable you to reach your maturity: but some of you will pass away, and some of you will be kept here until the age of senility, such that they know nothing of what they knew before. And you see the earth lifeless, but then We shower water on it, and it stirs and swells and produces every beautiful species.[6]

—QUR'AN 22:5

We have indeed created man in the best of molds, but then do We return him to the lowest of the low; except those who believe and do righteous deeds, for they shall have a reward without end.[7]

—QUR'AN 95:4–6

8 Underappreciating the value and transient nature of time is a common pitfall in the human condition. Symptoms of this disease are found in constant states of procrastination, laziness, and heedlessness, in which we take time for granted and wander the earth without aim or purpose. In fact, it is the lure of immortality and endless time that caused Adam, the human archetype, to slip into a state of forgetfulness (Qur'an 7:20). The Qur'an offers a way out of this human condition by telling us to gain certainty in our belief in God, and then to act on that certainty by dedicating our lives to doing good works. In doing so, there will be obstacles and seductions that seek to take us away from the path, and therefore it is important for us to join with others who are committed to seeking and practicing the truth in order to strengthen ourselves in patience and perseverance.

9 Muslims, like Christians, believe in the second coming of Jesus as a sign that the final hour is near. However, Muslims believe that Jesus will return as a follower of Prophet Muhammad confirming the truth of God's absolute Oneness and the path of surrender to the will of God. Muslims also believe that when Jesus returns there will be an anti-Christ (*Ad-Dajjal* in Arabic) to challenge and oppose him, his way, and his message. As such, a common supplication that Muslims make is invoking God to protect them from the misguidance and temptation of the anti-Christ. There are various interpretations among Muslim scholars as to whether the anti-Christ will take the form of a human being, an institution, or a social construct that is antithetical to the way of the prophets.

10 This prophetic saying is meant to motivate us to take full advantage of our time on this earth by increasing the doing of good works, particularly before we are overtaken by any sort of trial or tribulation that could make it difficult, if not impossible, to perform these acts of worship and goodness.

Through the passage of time, verily human beings are in a state of loss, except those who have faith, and do righteous deeds, and join together in the mutual enjoining of truth, and of patient perseverance.[8]

—QUR'AN 103

Hasten to do good deeds before you are overtaken by one of the seven afflictions. Are you waiting for such poverty as will make you unmindful of devotion, or such prosperity as will make you corrupt, or such illness as will disable you, or such senility as will make you mentally unstable, or death as will overtake you suddenly, or for the anti-Christ[9] who is the worst apprehended, or the final hour, and the hour will be most grievous and most bitter.[10]

—PROPHET MUHAMMAD

To each is a goal to which God turns him; then strive together [as in a race] toward all that is good. Wherever you are, God will bring you together, for God has power over all things.

—QUR'AN 2:148

11 There is a great deal of emphasis placed on preferring the eternal life of the hereafter to the temporary deceptive life of the present world—the idea being that short-term sacrifices of unlawful pleasures (such as fornication or adultery) lead to long-term gain and satisfaction; whereas divulging in short-term pleasures may very well lead to long-term agony and loss.

12 Death is one of the few things in life that we can be certain of because no created being lives forever. A reminder of this reality forces us to focus our attention on the task at hand knowing that we have only so long to fulfill the purpose of our lives. As such, there tends to be a sense of urgency in the teachings of Prophet Muhammad, who said, "Be in the world as if you were a stranger or wayfarer," meaning that you should not become too attached to the fleeting life of this world to the neglect of those things that will give you success in the hereafter.

13 This is a prophetic reminder that the only thing truly worthy of accumulating in this world is the doing of good deeds that will help us gain entry into paradise in the hereafter. All else, whether it is money or fame, will leave us at the graveside and be of no benefit to us in the world to come.

Know that the life of the world is but diversion and distraction, and ostentation and boasting among yourselves, and striving for more and more property and children. It is like rain whose growth pleases the tillers, then dies out and you see it turn yellow, and then it crumbles. In the hereafter there is severe agony, and forgiveness from God, and divine acceptance. So what is the world but the stuff of deception? Race, then, to forgiveness from your Lord, and a garden spacious as heaven and earth, arranged for those who believe in God and the messengers of God. That is the bounty of God, which God bestows on whomever God will; and God is the possessor of the greatest bounty.[11]

—QUR'AN 57:20–21

Everyone will taste death.[12] And you will be paid your due on the Day of Resurrection. And whoever is kept away from the fire and admitted to the garden has gained salvation. And the life of this world is but the enjoyment of deception.

—QUR'AN 3:185

Three things follow a dead body: members of his family, his possessions, and his deeds. Two of them return and one remains with him. His family and his possessions return; his deeds remain with him.[13]

—PROPHET MUHAMMAD

14 This is one of the many passages found in the Qur'an that describes in masterful language what will occur when the last hour is upon us. The first trumpet, sounded by an angel, will cause the destruction and end of all living creation. Then, the angel will blow another trumpet and all that ever lived will be resurrected by God. Then, each soul will be brought forth for questioning and God will pass judgment in accordance with what is true and just.

15 "Guardians over you" refers to the two angels that sit on the right and left shoulder of every human being. The task of the angel on the right side is to record all our good deeds; the task of the angel on the left side is to record all our bad deeds. This scroll of deeds for each of us is then presented before God on the Day of Accountability.

No just estimate have they made of God, in whose grip the whole earth will be on the Day of Requital, and in whose right hand the heavens will be rolled up. Glory to God, high above any partners they associate! And the trumpet will be sounded, when all in the heavens and on earth will lose consciousness, except whomever God wills. Then a second one will be sounded, when, behold, they will be standing, looking on. And the earth will shine with the light of its Lord, and the record will be set out, and the prophets and the witnesses will be brought forward, and judgment among them will be made, according to truth, and they shall not be wronged in the least. And every soul will be recompensed for what it did; and God knows best all that they do.[14]

—QUR'AN 39:67–70

When the sky splits, and when the stars are scattered, and when the oceans are drained, and when the graves are turned upside down, shall each soul know what it has produced and what it has left undone. O human being! What has seduced you from your generous Lord who created you, fashioned you in due proportion, and gave you a just bias, forming you in any form at will? Nay, but instead you deny the judgment, though there are guardians over you, honorable, keeping records, who know what you do.[15] As for the righteous, they will be in bliss. And the wicked, they will be in the fire, which they will enter on the Day of Requital. And what will explain to you what the Day of Requital is? Again, what will explain to you what the Day of Requital is? The day when no soul shall have the power to do anything for another; for the matter that day is wholly up to God.

—QUR'AN 82

16 This is reference to one of the most heinous crimes, female infanticide, which was common practice in pre-Islamic Arabia and continues
to exist in certain parts of the world today. Such evil will not go unpun-
ished on the Day of Requital.

17 Our questioning by God on the Day of Accountability will consist primarily of our performance as a deputy of God on earth, and whether
we fulfilled the trust and covenant of life. Much of this will depend on
how we used the great and unique intellectual gifts given to us by God;
whether we spent our wealth for good purposes, such as feeding the
poor, or wasted it in love of materialism; and for what end we used
our limbs—for the sake of performing good actions or spreading evil
and destruction.

When the sun is folded up, and when the stars fall lusterless, and when the mountains crumble, and when the pregnant camels are left untended, and when the wild beasts are herded together, and when the oceans are flooded, and when the souls are sorted out, and when the infant girl who was buried alive will ask for what crime she was killed,[16] and when the scrolls are laid open, and when the sky is unveiled, and when the blazing fire is kindled to fierce heat, and when the garden is brought near; then shall each soul know what it has brought forward.

—QUR'AN 81:1–14

A servant of God will remain standing on the Day of Requital till he is questioned about his life on earth and how he spent it, and about his knowledge and how he utilized it, and his wealth and how he acquired it and in what did he spend it, and about his body and how he used it.[17]

—PROPHET MUHAMMAD

O humanity, be in awe of your Lord! For the convulsion of the [Final] Hour will be a thing terrible!

—QUR'AN 22:1

Men ask thee concerning the [Final] Hour: Say, "The knowledge thereof is with God alone." And what will make you understand that perhaps the [Final] Hour is near!

—QUR'AN 33:63

18 This passage illustrates to us with powerful imagery the contrasting destinations of those who spread corruption on earth and those who do good in the world. The former will regret the course of their lives and wish they had devoted themselves to God. The latter will rejoice in a state of peaceful tranquility, having made the right moral choices in life.

19 We have been given temporary mastery over our own body, which is forced to do whatever we make it do. However, the body, as a creation of God, naturally inclines toward worshiping and serving God. So anytime we use our bodies for disobeying God, we are in fact oppressing it by opposing its very nature. On the Day of Requital, the body is given the right to speak against us—in perfect justice—as a victim of our rebellion against God.

The rejecters of faith will be led in groups to hell, until, when they arrive there, its gates will be opened, and its keepers will say, "Did not messengers come to you from among yourselves, rehearsing to you the messages of your Lord, and warning you of the meeting on this day of yours?" The answer will be, "Yes, but the decree of punishment has been proven just for the rejecters of faith." They will be told, "Enter you the gates of hell, to dwell therein, and what a miserable abode it is for the arrogant." As for those who were conscious of their Lord, they will be led to the garden in groups, until behold, they arrive there, its gates will be opened, and its keepers will say, "Peace be upon you, well have you done! Enter you here, to dwell therein." They will say, "Praise be to God, who has truly fulfilled the divine promise to us, giving us the land in inheritance, we can dwell in the garden as we will, how excellent a reward for those who work [righteous deeds]!" And you will see the angels surrounding the throne of God on all sides, singing glory and praise to their Lord. The decision between them will be in perfect justice, and the cry will be, "Praise be to God, the Lord of the worlds!"**18**

—QUR'AN 39:71–75

The day the opponents of God will be gathered together to the fire, they will be marched in ranks. At length, when they reach there, their hearing, their sight, and their skins will bear witness against them about what they used to do. And they will say to their skins, "Why did you testify against us?" They will say, "God has given us speech, Who gives speech to everything, Who created you for the first time, and to Whom you will return. You did not seek to hide yourselves, lest your hearing, your sight, and your skins should bear witness against you, but you supposed that God does not know much of what you do. But this thought of yours which you entertained concerning your Lord, has brought you to destruction, and now you have become of those utterly lost."**19**

—QUR'AN 41:19–23

20 This passage is one of many throughout the Qur'an that offer a vivid description of paradise and hellfire, with paradise being a place of beauty and pleasure, and hellfire a place of fear and pain. There is much discussion and debate among the commentators of the Qur'an as to what extent these descriptions are literal and to what extent they are metaphorical. Literalist-leaning interpretations say that God only speaks the truth and to deny the reality of any of these descriptions is to accuse God of untrue promises. Metaphorical-leaning interpretations argue that in reality the bliss of paradise and the torment of hell are beyond human perception and human language, and therefore these descriptions of the hereafter are meant to instill longing and fear within us for something that cannot be truly perceived.

21 It is essential for us to know that as much as the Day of Requital will be a manifestation of divine justice, it will also be a manifestation of divine mercy and forgiveness. In fact, according to the Islamic tradition, no one can gain entry into paradise without divine mercy and forgiveness, because the reality is that all of us sin and all of us fall short of our responsibilities as deputies of God on earth. Belief in God and doing good works place us in a better position to earn the divine mercy and forgiveness needed to pass the test, but in the end God chooses to forgive whomever God wants, knowing best what is hidden in the hearts of us all. Muslims look to some of the following passages from the Qur'an as a way of gaining hope in God's Mercy: "My Mercy embraces all things" (7:156); "Inform my servants that I am indeed the Forgiving, the Merciful" (15:49); "Say: O my servants, who have transgressed against their own soul, despair not of God's Mercy, for God forgives all sins, (and) God is the Forgiving, the Merciful" (39:53).

22 The only unpardonable sin according to the Qur'an is associating partners with God and worshiping anything else besides God. This need not take the form of an idol or a human being, but can also take the form of our own lower desires or extreme love for something, such as wealth, to the point that it becomes the central focus of our life and consciousness, taking up the position that must rightfully be reserved for God.

The description of the garden which the righteous are promised: In it are rivers of water which time does not corrupt; rivers of milk of which the taste never changes; rivers of wine, a joy to those who drink; and rivers of honey pure and clear. In it there are for them all kinds of fruits, and forgiveness from their Lord. Compare this to such as shall dwell forever in the fire, and are given to drink boiling water, so that it lacerates their guts.[20]

—QUR'AN 47:15

God created one hundred parts of mercy on the day the heavens and the earth were created. Each part contains all that is between the heavens and the earth. Of them, God put one part on the earth, by virtue of which a mother has compassion for her children and animals and birds have compassion for one another. On the Day of Requital, God will perfect and complete divine mercy.[21]

—PROPHET MUHAMMAD

God forgives not that a partner should be ascribed to God, but God forgives all else to whomever God will.[22]

—QUR'AN 4:48

1 In general we human beings tend to approach our particular state or condition in life with two types of psyche. The first looks at the great blessings around us, especially when there are many, and thinks of ourselves—consciously or subconsciously—as a divinely favored person or people, and becomes proud or arrogant in the process. Instead of showing gratitude to God for our blessings, we start attributing our successes to our own intellectual, physical, moral, and cultural superiority. This path that the human psyche often takes can be termed "the egotistic psyche."

2 The second type of psyche focuses on all that we are deprived of in this world, falling into a state of depression and despair, thinking that God has abandoned or dishonored us. Such a psyche can be called "the despairing psyche." Both types of psyche are archetypical responses to the human condition, but in the end they represent unhealthy and unbeneficial ways of thinking. In reality, both blessings and deprivations serve as ways to grow in faith and character (18:7–8). Similar to Buddhist teachings on the Middle Way, "right perception" and "right attitude" are necessary to make good moral decisions in life.

3 In the Islamic tradition, the heart is known as "the organ of perception," meaning that we tend to view the world based on the spiritual condition of our hearts. When the spiritual heart is diseased with arrogance, jealousy, hatred, and other illnesses, our ability to perceive divine reality and truth becomes more and more difficult. But when the ailments of the spiritual heart are removed, or at least tempered, our hearts gain an innate ability to see reality as reality, or as Buddhists would put it, we gain "pure consciousness." The following *hadith* summarizes this concept best: "Beware! There is a piece of flesh in the body. If it is healthy, the whole body is healthy. If it becomes unhealthy, the whole body becomes unhealthy. Verily, this flesh is the heart."

7 □ On the Psyche, Heart, and Soul

And as for man, whenever his Guardian-Lord tests him by honoring him and blessing him, he says, "My Guardian-Lord has honored me!"[1] And when his Guardian-Lord tests him by restricting his provision, he says, "My Guardian-Lord has humiliated me!"[2]

—QUR'AN 89:15–16

Haven't they traveled the earth, so that they may have hearts to understand, or ears to hear? Surely it is not their eyes that are blind; what is blind are the hearts that are in their breasts.[3]

—QUR'AN 22:46

On people's hearts is the stain of that which they do!

—QUR'AN 83:14

When a servant commits a sin, a dark spot appears upon his heart. If he desists, seeks forgiveness and makes repentance, then his heart is cleansed. And if he returns [to the sin], it [the dark spot] is increased until it takes over the heart, and this is the 'covering' that God mentions [83:14].

—PROPHET MUHAMMAD

4 The worst possible state of being is one in which people are so engrossed in their own ego that they cut off all their spiritual sensory input so that nothing in the way of guidance—no matter how clear—penetrates the layers and layers of darkness that separate the heart from divine light (Qur'an 24:40). Such a state is caused by persistent sinning, arrogance, and heedlessness (83:14). This type of soul is referred to as "the evil inclining soul" (*nafs al-ammarah bis-sou*). Those who have attained such a state are referred to in the Qur'an as *kaafir*. Unfortunately this word is often wrongly translated as "disbeliever," "unbeliever," or "infidel." However, *kaafir* denotes a much more active form of rejecting, hiding, or mocking the truth. A more accurate translation of *kaafir* is "those who reject faith," "those who hide truth," or "the mockers of faith." It is these particular perceptions and attitudes against faith that the Qur'an condemns and warns against.

5 This is a state in which the soul is constantly wavering between faith and disbelief depending on the tide of the moment. If this constantly wavering state persists in the soul, it inevitably leads to one of the worst spiritual states: hypocrisy. The Qur'an warns extensively about the peril of hypocrisy and the evil that it leads to (2:8–20). Hypocrisy is the self-deluded idea that we can live on both sides of the fence whenever it suits our situation. In reality this is just another way of serving and satisfying lower desires, which inevitably lead to undesirable outcomes in this world and the afterlife.

6 The door to repentance, change, and self-purification is always open to everyone, no matter how much they have strayed and no matter how much evil they have done. God forgives all sins, according to the Qur'an and many sayings of Prophet Muhammad. So even if a person falls into one of the undesirable states of being, there is always hope, so long as that person does not refuse the lifeboat handed to them in the form of repentance (*tawba*).

And We have created many of the sprites and humans for hell: they have hearts, but they do not understand thereby; and they have eyes, but do not see thereby; and they have ears, but do not hear thereby. They are like cattle, but even more astray; they are heedless.[4]

—QUR'AN 7:179

Some people worship God as it were on the verge: If something good happens to them, they are satisfied with it, but when a trial happens to them, they turn on their faces.[5] They lose this world and the hereafter; that is truly a loss.

—QUR'AN 22:11

[Those] who repent and attain to faith, and act with righteousness—in their case God transforms their evil into good, for God is most forgiving, most merciful. And whoever repents and does good is turning to God repentant.[6]

—QUR'AN 25:70–71

[7] When God swears by something in the Qur'an it is considered to be mighty and significant in value. The self-reproaching soul (*nafs al-lawwamah*) acts in good faith as the moral conscience in the battle between good and evil. This soul recognizes and criticizes its shortcomings and strives to overcome them in an effort to achieve the "tranquil soul."

[8] In removing ailments from the spiritual heart, the goal is to decorate it with the beauty of God-consciousness. This is achieved through praying, devotional chanting, charity, fasting, and other spiritual disciplines. When the heart is filled with God-consciousness it naturally inclines toward all those qualities and virtues that strengthen the spiritual heart, such as kindness and generosity. When the heart reaches a state in which God-consciousness rules over heedlessness, a person enters into a station (state of soul) of God-conscious (*mutaqeen*).

[9] The term *aslama* in Arabic is a variation of the word *muslim*, both of which mean "surrender to divine will." *Muslim,* as much as it is considered a category of people who follow Islam, is used more often in the Qur'an to describe the proper state of being in relation to God. In this sense, those who surrender and devote themselves wholly to God are in a state of Islam.

[10] In this passage the Qur'an makes a distinction in states of being between someone who surrenders his or her will to God (*muslim*) and someone who also has complete faith and trust in God (*mu'min;* pl. *mu'mineen*). A Muslim can practice all the outward motions of prayer, good works, and whatever else is divinely enjoined, while at the same time have some doubt about faith in his or her heart. Yet, a higher state of being is to be a *mu'min*—someone who has complete faith, trust, and certainty in the heart and who also surrenders his or her whole being to God. In terms of states of being, a *muslim* cannot be a *mu'min,* whereas a *mu'min* is necessarily also a *muslim*. It can be understood in terms of an upward motion, with *muslim* being the essential foundation and *mu'min* being the next level or state.

And I swear by the self-reproaching soul.[7]

—QUR'AN 75:2

The home of the hereafter We will give to those who do not desire exaltation on earth, or immorality. And the result is for the God-conscious [mutaqeen].[8]

—QUR'AN 29:83

And who is better in faith than the one who willingly surrenders his being to God [aslama wajhahoo],[9] and is a doer of good, and follows the way of Abraham the rightly oriented? For God took Abraham as a friend.

—QUR'AN 4:125

The desert Arabs say, "We believe" [amana]. Say, "You don't believe, you only say, 'We willingly surrender to God' [aslamna], for complete faith [iman] has not yet entered your hearts.[10] Yet, if you obey God and God's messenger, God will not deny you the reward for your deeds; for God is very forgiving, most merciful.

—QUR'AN 49:14

11 This is one of many verses that speak of the highly regarded *muhsin* (pl. *muhsineen*), which is a state of being that surpasses even that of a *mu'min*. *Muhsin* is such a deep state that it is difficult to translate. English translations thus far have described *muhsin* as "doer of good" or "righteous." While these meanings are true of a *muhsin*, they are severely lacking, in my opinion, in their description of what a *muhsin* truly is. The term in Arabic comes from two root words, *hasana* and *hasuna*, meaning "excellent" and "beautiful." Hence, I have described the *muhsin* state of being as "beautifully excellent devotees." A *muhsin* is someone who is in a constant state of worship, seeking to do good wherever he or she is, and in doing so making the world a more beautiful and excellent place of living for others. One who is a *muhsin* is also necessarily a *muslim* and a *mu'min*, having reached the next highest state of being.

12 The greatest station a soul can achieve in this world and in the afterlife is the "tranquil soul" (*al-nafs al-mutma'innah*), which is in complete harmony and tranquility with God. Achieving this takes a lifetime of devotion and dedication to spiritual development, and it is usually only fully realized toward the end of a devotee's life. It is, without doubt, the most desired and loftiest of stations for the soul in Islamic spirituality.

And be patient, for God will not neglect the reward of the beautifully excellent devotees [*muhsin*].**11**

—QUR'AN 11:115

O tranquil soul, return to your Guardian-Lord, pleased and accepted: enter the company of My servants; enter into My garden.**12**

—QUR'AN 89:27–30

Beautifully excellent devotion [*ihsan*] is that you worship God as if you see God; for if you do not see God then [at least know that] truly God sees you.

—PROPHET MUHAMMAD

Those who have faith and do righteous deeds, they are the best of creatures. Their reward is with God: Gardens of Eternity, beneath which rivers flow; they will dwell therein forever; God is well pleased with them, and they [are well pleased] with God: all this is for all those in awe of their Guardian-Lord.

—QUR'AN 98:7–8

1 Your spiritual devotion must begin with reflection, for it is in the reflection of divine signs that you will discover an intimate relationship with God's beautiful attributes. It is interesting to consider that Prophet Muhammad's own journey toward God began not with revelation, but with nights of deep reflection, meditation, and contemplation. The Qur'an also recounts the story of Prophet Abraham coming to a state of certainty and realization concerning the Oneness of God after reflecting on the marvelous creation of the heavens. A common saying among people of inward purification is, "Reflection is the lamp of the heart; if it is abandoned the heart will have no light." Given these teachings on reflection, Muslims have a practice known as *itikaf,* or "spiritual retreat," in which they leave behind all worldly affairs for a few days and nights to spend time reading scripture, prophetic stories, and other sacred texts that inspire closeness to God.

2 Remembrance of divine gifts, such as the food we have to eat and the family we seek comfort in, is a form of spiritual practice that focuses more on recalling or reminding our soul of those things that will cause it to render thanks to God. Muslims engage in this form of spiritual practice by saying "Praise and thanks is due to God," invoked in Arabic as *"Allhamdulillah,"* after each prayer, upon hearing good news, upon finishing a meal, and so on.

3 The act of remembering God in your heart or out loud results in God's remembrance of you, just as the beloved responds to the call of his or her devotee. Muslims seek to develop this intimate relationship with their Beloved by engaging in constant praise (*dhikr*) of divine attributes, either silently inward or out loud in group chanting, usually mentioning each invocation thirty-three or ninety-nine times and using either their fingers or beautifully crafted beads to keep count. There is thought to be special blessings if this remembrance is done in the early hours between the morning prayers (*fajr*) and sunrise (*shuruq*) or during the last third of the night, in which Prophet Muhammad said that God comes down to the lowest heaven and seeks out the servants who ask for divine forgiveness of their sins and providence for their affairs.

8 □ On Spiritual Practice and Discipline

On the earth are signs for those of assured faith, as also in your own selves; will you not then see?[1]

—QUR'AN 51:20–21

Remember the favors of God, so that you may succeed.[2]

—QUR'AN 7:69

Should you attempt to count the favors of God, you would not be able to do so.

—QUR'AN 45:18

Remember Me and I shall remember you. Be grateful to Me, and reject not faith.[3]

—QUR'AN 2:152

4   The defining result of remembering God is that your heart is filled
with peace and tranquility as it listens to the praise of its Creator and
Sustainer. This is why it is particularly common for Muslims to engage
in the spiritual practice of remembrance during times of hardship, distress, or grief—to bring calmness to a perturbed heart. However, a
noble devotee will remember his or her Beloved during both good and
bad times. Remembrance can also take the form of listening to recitation of the Qur'an, religious music, chanting, or the like.

5   One of the most spiritually refreshing practices you can benefit from
is a washing called *wudu* in Arabic. This spiritual and physical cleansing
can be performed at any time of the day and must be performed before
every prayer. It is a short ritual that can be performed anywhere you
have access to water. *Wudu* begins with an intention to purify your
heart by simply stating, "In the Name of God, the Merciful, the Compassionate." After this, the washing consists of the following steps: First,
wash your hands three times. Second, rinse your mouth three times.
Third, sniff some water into your nose three times. Fourth, wash your
whole face three times. Fifth, wash your right and left arms up to your
elbows three times. Sixth, take your wet hands and wipe them over
your head, around your neck, and in the inner and outer parts of your
ears. Seventh, wash your right and left feet up to your ankles three
times. The *wudu* is completed by offering a short supplication, the most
common of which is, "O God, make us among those who return to You,
and make us among those who purify themselves." The result of your
washing will be that it makes you physically fresh and clean in order to
be more attentive in your worship and devotions. Furthermore, the
wudu is a spiritual cleansing and purification of sins that any part of your
body may have committed between one prayer and another.

It is in the remembrance of God that hearts do find satisfaction.[4]

—QUR'AN 13:28

O you who believe, when you prepare for prayer, wash your faces, and your hands and arms to the elbows, and wipe your head, and your feet to the ankles. And if you are in a state of ceremonial impurity, then bathe your whole body. But if you are ill, or on a journey, or one of you comes from the call of nature, or you have been intimate with women, and you cannot obtain water, then get yourselves fine earth or sand and wipe your faces and hands with it. God does not wish hardship for you, but wants to make you pure, and to complete divine favor on you, so you may be grateful.[5]

—QUR'AN 5:6

6 │ After your spiritual washing in the form of *wudu*, you are ready to begin the prescribed prayers, known in Arabic as *salat*. This passage alludes to the five obligatory prayers that Muslims perform at different periods of the day and night. The first prayer, known as *fajr*, comes in the early morning before sunrise. The second prayer, known as *dzhur*, comes when the day begins to decline, just after noon. The third prayer, known as *'asr*, is offered in the late afternoon, between noon and sunset. The fourth prayer, known as *maghrib*, comes in just after sunset. The final fifth prayer, known as *'isha*, is offered after the evening twilight has completely faded from the horizon, and night has set in. The prayers are spread out so that throughout the day, in the midst of work and enjoyment, Muslims are constantly drawn back to what should be at the center of their lives—the remembrance and praise of God.

When the Muslim—or believing—servant of God does *wudu'* and washes his face, every wrong thing at which his eyes have looked leaves with the water—or with the last drop of water. When he washes his hands, every wrong thing which his hands have touched leaves with the water—or with the last drop of water. When he washes his feet, every wrong thing to which his feet have walked leaves with the water—or with the last drop of water, until he emerges cleansed of sins.

—Prophet Muhammad

And establish regular prayers at the two ends of the day and at the approaches of the night; for those things that are good remove those that are bad. That is a reminder for the mindful.[6]

—Qur'an 11:114

7 The night hours are a special time for devoting yourself to God because of the solitude and quietude of such prayers, which allow for minimal distractions from the remembrance of God. The Qur'an singles out for elite praise the ones who "shun their beds as they pray to their Lord in fear and hope" (32:16).

8 Your prayer itself consists of the following physical and spiritual motions: First, raise your hands to your ears while saying, "God is the Greatest." Second, release your hands to the side or clasp them on your stomach while remaining in a standing position where you recite the opening chapter of the Qur'an and any other Qur'anic passage of your liking. Third, after completing the recitation of passages, go into the bowing position and say, "Glory be to God, the Most High," at least three times. Fourth, return to the standing position while saying, "God hears all praises," and "To our Lord is all praise due." Fifth, go into a complete prostration with your forehead and nose touching the earth; in this position again say, "Glory be to God, the Most High," at least three times. After a brief sitting, go back into the prostrating position and then return to the standing position for another cycle to begin. Each prayer has a different number of cycles, and in each there is a short period of sitting in which you renew the testimony of faith ("There is no deity worthy of worship except God, and Muhammad is the messenger of God") and send peace and blessings upon Abraham and his followers and upon Muhammad and his followers. To end the prayer, turn your face to the right and say, "Peace be upon you, and God's Mercy"; repeat the same thing as you turn your face to the left.

9 In taking time out to remember and worship God at least five times a day, you gain a sense of divine awareness and consciousness at all times and places that allows you to repel any of your bad qualities or habits and embrace those qualities that are good and pleasing in the sight of God. This is the very transforming purpose and nature of prayer in your life.

[And the servants of the Merciful are] those who spend the night[7] in adoration of their Lord prostrating and standing.[8]

—QUR'AN 25:64

Recite what is sent of the book by inspiration to you, and establish regular prayer; for prayer restrains from repulsive and evil conduct. And remembrance of God is even greater. And God knows what you do.[9]

—QUR'AN 29:45

The similitude of the five prayers is that of a flowing river at the door of one of you in which he washes five times every day.

—PROPHET MUHAMMAD

10 Friday, during the hours of *dzhur* prayer, Muslims congregate in mosques throughout the world to listen to a religious sermon followed by congregational prayers. This is similar to attending something like Catholic Mass on Sundays. The sermon usually reminds believers of their duties before God and toward fellow human beings, and encourages them to practice goodness and shun evil. For you, this spiritual practice is meant as a time for deep reflection and introspection on how you spent the week and on the general direction of your soul—whether it is journeying closer to God or moving away from God.

11 In this passage, the Qur'an discourages two types of extremes. The first is completely abandoning the world and all worldly affairs to the point that you do not even make a living for yourself and your family. The second is indulging so much in business, materialism, and other worldly affairs that you end up abandoning God and do not fulfill even the most basic religious duties and obligations. The best path is to make time for prayer and other religious duties, to make time for business and other worldly affairs, and to always remember and be mindful of God.

12 In this passage, God speaks directly in the first person "I" and "Me" to emphasize the closeness of the Creator to the created and to encourage us to offer supplications for divine providence. The spiritual practice of offering supplications or asking God allows us to draw nearer to the Merciful One and to recognize our state of humbleness and poverty before the Rich and Generous One. As such, it is recommended that we ask God by raising our open hands before ourselves as a beggar would do in the presence of the rich.

O you who believe, when the call is proclaimed to prayer on Friday, hasten earnestly to the remembrance of God, and leave all worldly affairs.[10] That is best for you if you but knew. And when the prayer is finished, then may you disperse through the land, and seek the bounty of God; and remember God abundantly so that you may prosper. But when they see some bargain or some pastime, they disperse headlong to it, and leave you standing. Say, "That which God has is better than any pastime or bargain, and God is the Best of Providers."[11]

—QUR'AN 62:9–11

When my servants ask you concerning Me, I am indeed near. I respond to the supplication of every supplicant when he calls on Me. Let them too, with a will, listen to My call, and believe in Me, so that they may walk in the right way.[12]

—QUR'AN 2:186

13 After the spiritual devotion of prayer comes the spiritual practice and discipline of giving to the poor and needy in the form of an annual obligatory alms tax, known as *zakat*. Interestingly, this Arabic word for almsgiving comes from a root word meaning "to purify." The idea here is that when you give alms you are in fact purifying your own soul of covetousness and purifying your wealth of any unlawfulness or excessive indulgence in materialism. As such, *zakat* is seen as a spiritual discipline as much as a way to bridge the gap between the wealthy and the needy.

14 Charity (known as *sadaqa* in Arabic) and the giving of gifts in reality benefit none other than your own soul, for in the act of giving you free yourself from the bondage of miserliness and materialism, which causes many to stray from God. Generosity is among the foremost qualities of God's devotees, and in being generous you draw yourself closer to the most Generous One, who will fulfill your needs just as you seek to fulfill the needs of others. While *zakat* is obligatory for every sufficiently wealthy Muslim, *sadaqa* is optional but highly recommended. And while *zakat* comes mainly in the form of material giving, *sadaqa* can also take the form of nonmaterial gifts, such as a smile or offering a helping hand.

And establish prayer and give alms, for whatever good you send forth for your souls, you will find it with God; for God sees well all that you do.**13**

—QUR'AN 2:110

So be conscious of God as much as you can by listening and obeying [God]. And spend in charity for the benefit of your own souls, for those saved from the covetousness of their own souls are the ones who achieve success. If you loan to God a good loan, God will multiply it for you, and forgive you; for God is most appreciative, most clement, Knower of what is hidden and what is open, the Almighty, the Wise.**14**

—QUR'AN 64:16–18

Increase the number of prostrations, for every prostration that you perform before God will raise your [spiritual] position one degree and will remove one of your sins.

—PROPHET MUHAMMAD

15 For Muslims, fasting consists, in its most elementary form, of abstaining from any food, drink, or sexual intimacy from sunrise to sunset. At a deeper level, fasting also means keeping your eyes, ears, tongue, hands, and feet from committing any sin or from doing anything that is displeasing to God. Fasting is a spiritual discipline that assists in developing a deeper, closer, and more intimate relationship and awareness of divine presence so that you are cognizant of your behavior in all aspects of life, whether in the open or in secret. You can fast during any time of the year, though it is encouraged especially on Mondays and Thursdays to follow the practice of Prophet Muhammad, and at least three times every month. The maximum you should fast is every other day, which was the practice of Prophet David. Fasting more than this is considered a disliked extreme, unless of course it is during the month of fasting, known as Ramadan.

16 The month of Ramadan is special because it is when the Qur'an was first revealed to Prophet Muhammad. As such, Muslims perform an obligatory fast during this month to show their gratitude and appreciation for scriptural guidance. The reason fasting is prescribed as a spiritual practice during this month, above all other spiritual practices, is because the very nature of fasting allows you to develop those qualities and virtues that are most highly spoken of in the Qur'an, such as patience, humbleness, self-restraint, compassion, and the like.

17 The result of your fasting should be that you learn to be more grateful for and appreciative of the gifts and blessings God has given you. In experiencing a temporary absence of life's most essential blessings, you become more aware of the many blessings you have and the gratitude you ought to show for these gifts.

O you who believe, fasting is prescribed to you as it was prescribed to those before you, so that you may be conscious of God.[15] ... Ramadan is the month in which the Qur'an was sent down, as a guide to humanity, and demonstrations in the way of guidance, and as a criterion. So whoever among you is present that month should fast.[16] If anyone is ill or on a journey, then the prescribed term is to be made up from other days. God wishes ease for you, not hardship; and that you fulfill the prescribed terms, and that you celebrate God for guiding you; and that you may be grateful.[17]

—Qur'an 2:183, 185

When any one of you is fasting on a day, he should neither indulge in obscene language nor should he raise his voice; and if anyone insults him or tries to quarrel with him, he should say, "I am fasting."

—Prophet Muhammad

If one does not abstain from lies and bad conduct, God has no need that he should abstain from his food and drink.

—Prophet Muhammad

18 This passage speaks of the annual pilgrimage to the holy city of Mecca, which Muslims must perform at least once in their lifetime if they are physically and financially able to do so. The pilgrimage consists of tracing the ancient footsteps and spiritual practices of Prophet Abraham, who Muslims believe built the *kabba,* or the House of God, with his son Ishmael. The crying call of pilgrims throughout the pilgrimage is, "Here I am before You, O God, at Your service. Before you I am, there is no partner unto You, at your service here I am." During these rites, Muslims circle the *kabba* seven times to pay their respect to God; walk seven times between two mountains, known as Safa and Marwa, to reenact the struggles and devotion of Hagar as she sought provision for her child Ishmael; journey to a place known as Arafat, where it is believed that all of humanity will be gathered on the Day of Requital, for deep reflection and introspection, asking God for the best of this world and the hereafter; and partake in a spiritual practice that entails a symbolic stoning of the devil to repel evil elements within human nature. During the pilgrimage, male pilgrims dress in two pieces of unstitched, long white towels wrapped around their upper and lower body, and women wear a plain long dress in order to remove any worldly distinctions of class or social position between the pilgrims. Pilgrims are prohibited from fighting, arguing, or killing even an ant. Pilgrimage is a journey that seeks to build the qualities of patience, sharing, kindness, and the like in your soul, even when such qualities are difficult to cultivate because of so many difficulties and hardships.

For pilgrimage are the months well-known. If anyone undertakes that duty therein, let there be no obscenity, nor wickedness, nor wrangling during pilgrimage. And whatever good you do, God knows it. And take a provision for the journey, but the best provision is God-consciousness. So be conscious of Me, O you that are wise.[18]

—QUR'AN 2:197

Whoever performs pilgrimage and does not have sexual relations, nor commits sins, nor disputes unjustly, then he returns from pilgrimage as pure and free from sins as on the day he was born.

—PROPHET MUHAMMAD

19 A spiritual discipline given to a few prophets in the Qur'an is the practice of remaining silent for an extended period of time. Practicing silence has many benefits for your soul, including disciplining of the tongue—an organ that has the potential for great good and great harm. The golden rule concerning the tongue in Prophet Muhammad's teaching is, "He who believes in God and the Last Day must either speak good or remain silent."

20 At the root of all spiritual practices and disciplines is the idea of struggling against our lower desires and passions, which act as obstacles in the path to God and as veils to your becoming fully aware of divine presence. None of our spiritual ambitions can be realized without making a concerted effort and having a strong determination to overcome the obstacles that we experience in our spiritual journey. Once we are committed to that struggle, God will guide us along the path and will aid us in our efforts.

[Zakariya] said, "O my Lord, give me a sign!" "Your sign," was the answer, "shall be that you speak to no man for three nights, although you are not deprived of speech."[19]

—QUR'AN 19:10

And those who strive for Our sake, We will certainly guide them to Our paths, for verily God is with those who do right.[20]

—QUR'AN 29:69

The Prophet's wife, Ayesha, said: "The Prophet would stand in prayer so long that the skin of his feet would crack." Ayesha asked the Prophet, "Why do you do this while your past and future sins have been forgiven?" The Prophet replied: "Should I not be a grateful servant of God?"

—PROPHET MUHAMMAD

A [spiritually] strong believer is better and dearer to God than a [spiritually] weak one in all good things. Adhere to that which is most [spiritually] beneficial for you. Keep beseeching God for help and do not refrain from it. If you are afflicted in any way, do not say: "If I had taken this or that step, it would have resulted in such and such," but say only, "God so determined and did as willed." The word *if* opens the gates of evil conduct.

—PROPHET MUHAMMAD

The hellfire is surrounded with all kinds of desires and passions, while paradise is surrounded with adversities.

—PROPHET MUHAMMAD

1 This is a prophetic saying that is directly inspired by God as a saying of God, known in the Islamic tradition as *hadith qudsi*. This saying focuses on one of the most important aspects of religious devotional life, namely the link between law and spirituality. Often these two concepts are considered juxtaposed to one another, with law being a rigid set of dos and don'ts that govern human life, and spirituality being a free movement of the soul in a way that rises above material concerns in order to reach imminence with the Transcendent One. However, in Islamic philosophy there is a real concerted effort to bridge the gap between notions of law and spirituality, seeking to build one whole, solid bridge that leads to God. Law is for the soul to come into sync with and in obedience to divine will; spirituality is for the soul to draw closer to God in an intimate friendship with love as its basis. In other words, the ultimate aspiration of both law and spirituality is one and the same, and the two work together to achieve congruent goals, just as the two wings of a bird work together to fly. Laws pertaining to daily life are found throughout the Qur'an and relate to governing our limbs, behavior, and social interactions.

2 Concerning the laws in daily life that you should guard most vigilantly are those commandments that have to do with your own heart and limbs. They are what you are most responsible for, and God has given you mastery over them. If you oppress your limbs by forcing them to do what they were not created for (disobeying God), then they will testify against you on the Day of Requital. If you use your limbs for what they were created to do (obey God), then they will testify on your behalf and in your favor on the day you meet God. The masters of Islamic spiritual sciences say that all the laws regarding your limbs are meant to protect your heart from corruption and nourish your heart toward goodness. There are seven limbs to your heart that act as regulating gates to keep out evil and to usher in purity, functioning like the gates of a city. These limbs are the eyes, ears, tongue, stomach, genitals, hands, and feet. Daily laws are focused on guarding and using each one of these limbs for you to draw closer to God in this world and in the afterlife.

9 □ On Laws in Daily Life

Prophet Muhammad said, God says, "Nothing brings men near to Me like the performance of what I have made obligatory for them; and through works of supererogation My servant comes ever nearer to Me until I love him, and when I have bestowed My love on him, I become his hearing with which he hears, his sight with which he sees, his tongue with which he speaks, his hands with which he grasps, and his feet with which he walks; and if he asks of Me, I give him, and if he asks My protection, I protect him."[1]

—DIVINE SAYING RELATED BY PROPHET MUHAMMAD

And do not occupy yourself with what you have no knowledge of; for every act of hearing, and of seeing, and the impulse of the heart will all be questioned.[2]

—QUR'AN 17:36

A wise man is the one who calls himself to account and does noble deeds to benefit him after death; and the foolish person is the one who submits to his temptations and desires, and seeks from God the fulfillment of those vain desires.

—PROPHET MUHAMMAD

3 You must protect your eyes from anything that would be displeasing in the sight of God, particularly lustful glances (Qur'an 30:31) that entertain immodest and unsanctioned behavior toward anyone of the same or opposite gender. You should also avoid looking at another human being with contempt or arrogance (Qur'an 31:18). Instead, focus your eyes inwardly on your own faults and shortcomings, for the Prophet Muhammad advises us that "should you become eager to mention another's faults, recall your own." Furthermore, use your eyes to witness the beautiful, wondrous creation of God, and see the stamp of divine Mercy in every instance of your eyes opening (Qur'an 30:50, 67:19), for in doing so you will draw near to God, and your eyes will act as a friend on the day when all deeds are accounted for.

4 The spiritual gates of the ears and the tongue are closely related in their protection and nourishment of the heart. Anything that is prohibited for your ears to listen to is prohibited for your tongue to articulate, and vice versa. Similarly, anything that is praiseworthy for your ears to listen to is praiseworthy for your tongue to articulate, and vice versa. This passage is the most comprehensive in dealing with the laws governing your ears and tongue, which must vigilantly guard against backbiting, ridiculing, jesting, and scoffing at other people. Other verses of the Qur'an warn against lying and false oaths (25:72), breaking promises (23:8), engaging in vain conversations (23:3), and self-justification (53:32). Sayings of Prophet Muhammad further prohibit wrangling and arguing, cursing, and invoking evil on creatures. Instead, you must lend your ears to recitation of scripture, prophetic teachings, wise counsel from the people of knowledge and insight, good company, and other such things that bring soundness to your heart and closeness to God (Qur'an 13:28). In the same way, you must use your tongue to benefit your own soul (such as mentioning the beautiful divine names) and to benefit those around you (such as imparting useful knowledge or confronting a tyrant). In this way, your ears and tongue facilitate an opening to God, and these two gates will testify on your behalf on the Day of Accountability.

God knows the treachery of the eyes, and what is concealed in the hearts.[3]

—QUR'AN 40:19

O you who believe, people should not mock other people, for these may be better than they are. And women should not mock other women, for these may be better than they are. And do not ridicule each other, or call each other by insulting nicknames. Evil is the name of impiety after achieving faith; and they who do not refrain are wrongdoers. O you who believe, avoid suspicion, for some suspicion is sin, and do not spy on each other, and do not defame each other in their absence. Would any of you like to eat the flesh of his dead brother? Nay, you would abhor it! So be conscious of God, for God is Oft-Returning, Most Merciful.[4]

—QUR'AN 49:11–12

5 Now we move to the gate of the stomach, which is there to give you enough energy to worship God and to fulfill your earthly duties, while at the same time protect you from physical and spiritual illnesses, such as gluttony and laziness. The first way to benefit from your stomach, and to avoid harm, is to remember at the beginning and end of every meal the gratitude you owe God for the sustenance you have been given. This can be expressed by beginning the meal with "In the name of God, the Compassionate, the Merciful" and ending the meal with "All praise is due to the Lord of the universe." In doing so, your very eating and drinking count as acts of worship and as means of drawing closer to God.

6 You must be very vigilant about what you let into your body, because what you eat will certainly affect your physical and spiritual state. For this reason, the general ruling of Muslim jurists regarding the consumption of meat is that you are prohibited from eating carnivorous and omnivorous animals, such as cats or dogs, since they may possess the diseases of their prey and undesirable spiritual qualities, such as aggressiveness, greediness, and so on. Herbivores are conditionally permissible. In another place the Qur'an expands on the categories of prohibited meat to include "the animal that has been strangled, or beaten to death, or killed by fall, or gored to death, or savaged by a beast of prey, except that which you may have slaughtered while it was still alive, and all that has been slaughtered on idolatrous altars" (5:3). Meats that pass these laws are certified as *halal* (permissible) either by endorsing agencies (such as the Islamic Society of North America in the United States) or simply on a trust-based system between sellers and buyers.

So eat of the sustenance that God has provided for you, lawful and wholesome; and be grateful for the favors of God, if it is God that you serve.**5** God has forbidden you only dead meat and blood, and the flesh of swine, and anything over which the name of other than God has been invoked.**6** But if anyone is compelled by necessity, without wanting to or being excessive, then God is Oft-Forgiving, Most Merciful.

—QUR'AN 16:114–115

The best food is that over which there are many hands.

—PROPHET MUHAMMAD

Say grace; eat with your right hand; and eat what is close at hand.

—PROPHET MUHAMMAD

7 It is important for your physical and spiritual well-being not to overeat because this may cause many diseases and can also make you lazy in worshiping God. The golden prophetic rule concerning the amount you eat is related in the following saying of Prophet Muhammad: "The son of Adam does not fill any vessel worse than his stomach; for the son of Adam a few mouthfuls are sufficient to keep his back straight. But, if you must fill it, then one-third for food, one-third for drink, and one-third for air."

8 The Qur'an teaches that one of the ways in which human beings most deviate from the remembrance and worship of their Lord is by indulging in their own lower passions and transgressing all due limits for the temporary gain of sexual gratification (Qur'an 25:43). The Qur'an says that true happiness and success are found in controlling your desires and sharing this special intimacy with the one you love and are committed to in a sacred relationship of marriage (23:5–7). For this reason, it is essential to be mindful of and to guard your chastity in every time and place, and to flee from anything that even encourages the thought of fornication or adultery. Islamic law has made certain provisions to protect a person from his or her lower desires, such as requiring modest dress and behavior between members of the opposite sex who are not related to each other (Qur'an 24:30–31) and prohibiting secluded, unaccompanied meetings between an unmarried, unrelated man and woman.

9 As indicated in the above prophetic saying, sexual intimacy between a husband and wife is actually considered to be an act of goodness for which a couple receives divine rewards. The Qur'an encourages couples to perform an act of worship before engaging in intimacy so that the experience is of a spiritual as well as a physical nature (2:223).

O Children of Adam … eat and drink, without being excessive, for God does not love those who are excessive.[7]

—QUR'AN 7:31

And do not come near adultery, for it is a shameful and an evil path.[8]

—QUR'AN 17:32

Prophet Muhammad said, "In the sexual act of each of you there is an act of good charity." The Companions replied, "O messenger of God! When one of us fulfils his sexual desire, will he be given a reward for that?" And he said, "Do you not think that were he to act upon it unlawfully, he would be sinning? Likewise, if he acts upon it lawfully he will be rewarded."[9]

—PROPHET MUHAMMAD

God removes faith from one who engages in illicit sex or consumes intoxicants just as a man removes his shirt when pulling it over his head.

—PROPHET MUHAMMAD

10   Remember that your hands were not created by the Creator in order to engage in destructive and evil acts, so guard your hands from partaking in anything that is harmful to yourself or to another of God's creation. The reality is that God gives you hands as a charitable trust for you to perform good deeds. And the highest of these deeds involving the hands is giving in charity to the poor, feeding the hungry, clothing the naked, building shelter for the homeless, assisting or defending the weak, and freeing the oppressed—all of which constitute "for the sake of God."

11   The feet are the last of the seven gates protecting and nourishing your heart, but perhaps the most in need of control and attention because they serve in physically taking you to places of good or evil. Therefore, avoid using your feet to pursue useless and evil activities, such as going to a bar or entering a casino. The best use of your feet is to travel in the pursuit of sacred knowledge and wisdom (Qur'an 22:46), to stand up against injustice (Qur'an 4:135), and to seek from the bounty of God, for yourself and your family, in a moderate and lawful manner (Qur'an 62:10).

12   This passage mentions some of the most important things that have been made unlawful for Muslims in the sacred law. Wine, gambling, idolatry, and divination all share a common trait, which is that their very nature is to indulge wants and desires in a way that makes a person neglectful of God and heedless of time. Consuming alcohol impairs the intellect, which makes it more difficult to make morally conscious decisions. Gambling makes a person a slave of money, materialism, and luck and creates discord between people. Both alcohol and gambling can easily lead to a form of idolatry, which is idolatry of the self, meaning that a person places his or her own desires before God's will. Manifest idolatry sets barriers and veils between the self and One God; and divination has the same result—trusting and relying on something other than God, who is the best of providers.

And spend for the sake of God, and make not your own hands contribute to destruction. And do good, for God loves those who do good.[10]

—QUR'AN 2:195

On the Day [of Requital] their tongues and their hands and their feet will testify against them about what they had been doing.[11]

—QUR'AN 24:24

O believers, wine and gambling and idolatry and divination are nothing but abomination from the work of Satan, so avoid them that you may prosper. Satan only wants to sow hostility and hatred among you with wine and gambling, and to hinder you from remembrance of God, and from prayer, so will you not then abstain?[12]

—QUR'AN 5:90–91

13 Money ethics is one of the most frequently mentioned concerns in the Qur'an and in the teachings of Prophet Muhammad. First, trade must not involve vain or harmful pursuits, such as drugs, pornography, weaponry, and the like. Second, the exchange should be mutually beneficial and fair, without any one party seeking to exploit the other. In the same spirit, the Qur'an also completely forbids stealing from others (5:38). Third, business competition should never become so unhealthy or be filled with such enmity that it leads to someone even entertaining the thought of murdering another for financial gain or committing suicide out of despair over money.

14 In the Qur'an, healthy consumption is permissible (2:186), while lavishness (17:27), miserliness (35:29), and wastefulness (6:141) are strongly discouraged. The pursuit of a livelihood (106), worldly satisfaction (42:36), and beautification (7:31) are all allowed as long as they do not distract you from your responsibilities toward others (102) and take you away from the remembrance of God (62:11).

15 In daily financial affairs guard against profiting from or contributing to usurious interest, for such financial transactions are strictly prohibited. In another place the Qur'an says that "God deprives usurious interest of blessing, and grants increase for charities" (2:276). In the books of *hadith* it is also reported that Prophet Muhammad cursed the one who accepts usurious interest, the one who pays it, those who record it, and those who stand witness to it. The reason is that this type of financial system contributes to a social divide between rich and poor in which the rich keep on profiting from usurious interest-based loans while the poor, who are unable to pay their debts, fall deeper and deeper into poverty. As such, profiting or contributing to a financial system that is economically unjust for the poor and weak in society is among the greatest sins one can commit (Qur'an 2:278–279). Since the modern financial system is based largely on usurious transactions, many scholars have permitted taking usurious loans for the basic necessities of life, such as housing, if absolutely no other alternative exists. Some scholars also permit such loans for secondary necessities, such as education.

O you who believe, do not consume wealth among yourselves in vain. But let there be trade by mutual good will. And do not kill yourselves, for God has been merciful to you.[13]

—QUR'AN 4:29

Let not your hand be tied to your neck, nor stretch it forth to its utmost reach, so that you become blameworthy and destitute.[14]

—QUR'AN 17:29

O you who believe, devour not usurious interest, doubled and multiplied; but be conscious of God that you may prosper.[15]

—QUR'AN 3:130

1 Possessing and exhibiting good character, morals, and manners are at the core of what it means to be a Muslim. Developing these qualities is a lifelong process and is studied as its own subject within the sciences of Islamic spirituality (*ilm ul-akhlaq*). The focus is on developing noble qualities in the soul, such as patience, kindness, and modesty, and breaking the bad habits of the soul, such as lying, harshness, and ingratitude. This chapter looks at some of the many noble characteristics and morals that the Qur'an and *hadith* encourage us toward.

2 For Muslims, Prophet Muhammad is the complete embodiment of what it means to have noble character and good morals. The Qur'an itself says about the Prophet, "And you do indeed have an exalted standard of character" (68:4). Muslims celebrate the Prophet's life as the best of lives ever lived by praising him in works of poetry, forms of music, beautiful calligraphy, and above all in attempting to emulate his dignified and compassionate ways. For this reason, the life of Prophet Muhammad serves as a role model for Muslims in every aspect of their lives to this day.

3 Sincerity is the key to all good deeds. To gain worldly and spiritual rewards or blessings for your righteous works and good character, your intentions must be solely for the sake of serving God and gaining God's good pleasure. In fact, the Qur'an says that good deeds without good intention are of no real significance in the sight of God (24:39). So if your intentions for doing good deeds are to gain wealth or impress other people, then that is all you will gain while being deprived of the great divine blessings that come with good deeds based on good intentions. Muslims purify their intentions before any act, beginning it with, "By the name of God, Most Merciful, Most Compassionate." However, real intentions lie in your heart, and God is well aware of what is in your heart.

10 □ On Noble Character and Good Morals

The Prophet was asked, "Which Muslim has the perfect faith?" He answered, "One who possesses the best moral character."[1]

—PROPHET MUHAMMAD

I have not been sent except to perfect noble character.[2]

—PROPHET MUHAMMAD

The reward of deeds depends upon the intentions, and a person will get the reward according to what he has intended....[3]

—PROPHET MUHAMMAD

Keep God in mind wherever you are; follow a wrong with a right that offsets it; and treat people courteously.

—PROPHET MUHAMMAD

Should you wish to act, ponder well the consequences. If good, carry on; if not, desist.

—PROPHET MUHAMMAD

4 At the root of all noble character and good morals are the doing of good and avoiding of mischief or corruption on the earth. Goodness can be achieved in many ways and it is not restricted to any one set of actions. Prophet Muhammad said, "Enjoined on every part of the human body is charity, every day in which the sun rises. Doing justice between two people is charity, and helping a man onto his animal and leading it is charity, and a good word is charity, and every step which is taken toward prayer is charity, and removing harmful things from the road is charity."

5 The nature and characteristic of every good deed can be defined by mercy, gentleness, and kindness. For this reason Prophet Muhammad said, "Whenever kindness is added to something, it adorns it; and whenever it is withdrawn from something, it leaves it defective."

6 At the root of undignified character and immoral behavior is the lack of modesty or shyness before God and fellow human beings (Qur'an 31:19). For this reason, modesty (*haya* can also be translated as "shyness") is a core part of the Islamic faith. In fact, Prophet Muhammad said, "Every religion has its special characteristics, and the chief characteristic of Islam is modesty." Developing modesty with God means making God part of your consciousness and awareness at all times. This is done primarily through consistent praying and fasting. Nurturing modesty before other human beings means not offending them by your tongue, deeds, or behavior as much as is possible. This is done by humbling yourself in the presence of others, dressing and behaving as you would in front of someone you truly revere, and being considerate of other people's needs before your own.

Be good, as God has been good to you, and seek not mischief in the land, for God loves not those who do mischief.[4]

—QUR'AN 28:77

God will not show mercy to the one who does not show mercy to others.[5]

—PROPHET MUHAMMAD

Among the words of the previous prophets that have reached people are, "If you feel no modesty [*haya*], then do as you wish."[6]

—PROPHET MUHAMMAD

Modesty is part of faith and faith is in paradise; but obscenity is a part of hardness of heart and hardness of heart is in hell.

—PROPHET MUHAMMAD

Modesty and faith are two that go together. If one is removed, the other is also removed.

—PROPHET MUHAMMAD

Modesty does not come into anything without adorning it.

—PROPHET MUHAMMAD

7   Respecting your parents comes only second to the reverence you must show to God and the prophets. Your gratitude should be expressed by speaking to them with gentleness and compassion, obeying them in matters that do not go against divine teachings, and taking care of them in their old age. Your mother must be given a special status and respect since she bore you through hardship and difficulty (46:15). Prophet Muhammad said, "Paradise lies beneath the feet of mothers."

8   Praying for your parents is one of the highest forms of supplication you can offer. The Prophet would offer a supplication for his parents after every prayer with the words, "O God, forgive our parents!" In the tradition of Prophet Abraham, we are told to pray for our parents even if they do not treat us well and even if they are ill disposed toward faith (Qur'an 26:86), because their treatment of us does not absolve us of our treatment of them. Even after their passing from this worldly life, your supplications continue to be a source of benefit for them.

9   Benevolent treatment of your family is among the highest virtues you can engage in. Just conduct between all your family members is essential in this respect (Qur'an 4:1). Due to the unfair treatment of women in many households throughout the world, it is particularly important to remember the prophetic saying, "Whosoever has a daughter and does not bury her alive, does not insult her, and does not favor his son over her, God will enter him into paradise." Cutting off ties with any family member is considered one of the greatest sins in the Islamic tradition, so be quick to forgive and forget.

10   Meaning that Prophet Muhammad is the best role model for how we should treat our families. It is well-known in the books of *hadith* that the Prophet would assist in household chores, mend his own shoes, wash his own clothes, and help his wives in every way possible despite the enormous responsibilities that came with being a teacher and community leader for his people. So good treatment of your family is following the best of the prophetic model.

Your Lord has decreed that you worship none other than God, and that you be kind to parents. Whether one or both of them attain old age in your lifetime, say not to them a word of contempt, nor repel them, but address them in an honorable manner.[7] And, out of compassion, lower to them [your] wings of humility, and say, "My Lord! Bestow on them your Mercy as they cherished me when I was young."[8]

—QUR'AN 17:23–24

The best among you is the one who is best toward his family,[9] and I am the best among you to my family.[10]

—PROPHET MUHAMMAD

Be conscious of God and treat your children with equality.

—PROPHET MUHAMMAD

11 We are enjoined to show respect and kindness to all, even to those who are strangers and have no direct blood ties with us. There is a common saying in the Islamic tradition that "a civilization is known best by the way it treats its elders and in the way it treats its young." Prophet Muhammad said, "No youth will honor an old person without God appointing one to honor them when they are old."

12 Taking care of the weakest members of society, such as orphans, widows, and slaves, is considered to be among the greatest of noble traits. Assisting them in their needs and elevating their position in society are akin to struggling in the path of God, according to Prophet Muhammad. It has been written, "The Prophet said, 'I, and the one who takes care of an orphan, whether from his own family or of others, will be in paradise like this' (and he pointed his forefinger and middle finger with a slight space between them [indicating their closeness])."

13 Kindness and compassion must also be shown toward the nonhuman world. For this reason it is completely prohibited to kill an animal simply for game or for purposes other than removing harm or sustaining human life. The Qur'an says that animals, like human beings, form communities (6:38) and have a way of praising God (24:41), and therefore they must be protected and cared for as guests of God on earth. Once the Prophet was told of a woman who locked her cat in a room and gave it no food until it died of starvation. Upon hearing this, the Prophet said that she was destined for hellfire because of her cruelty. Also, the Prophet narrates the story of a prostitute who saw a thirsty dog and gave it water from a well to drink. For this kind act, God forgave all her sins and admitted her to paradise.

He who does not respect his elders and does not show love for the young ones is not from amongst us.[11]

—PROPHET MUHAMMAD

And [the righteous] feed, for the love of God, the indigent, the orphan, and the captive, [saying]: "We feed you for the sake of God alone. No reward do we desire from you nor thanks. We only fear a day of frowning and distress from the side of our Lord."[12]

—QUR'AN 76:7–10

Whoever kills a sparrow for no reason, it will cry out loud to God on the Day of Resurrection, saying: "O my Lord! This person killed me for no reason; he did not kill me for any good reason."[13]

—PROPHET MUHAMMAD

Verily, there is heavenly reward for every act of kindness done to a living animal.

—PROPHET MUHAMMAD

14 Lying is one of the greatest sins in Islam, and one of the greatest forms of lying is hypocrisy—when a person says one thing and does another (61:2–3). Hypocrisy is one of the most condemned states of being in the Qur'an. And fraud is one of the worst forms of deception (83:1–6). Speaking the truth and standing up for the truth, however, are qualities possessed by the people of righteousness. Truthfulness also requires maintaining oaths and promises and the fulfillment of all such obligations (Qur'an 5:1).

15 Patience, perseverance, and constancy are necessary virtues to have in order to live a good, moral life. This involves: enduring hardship and suffering while maintaining trust in God (Qur'an 2:155–157); keeping the soul from all reprehensible deeds and behavior that God has made prohibited; and relying on God for the final outcome of all efforts and supplications.

16 One of the greatest forms of patience is controlling your anger and being able to forgive others for their shortcomings. Prophet Muhammad warned greatly against anger, once pulling aside one of his young companions and advising him, "Do not be angry, do not be angry, do not be angry." Another time, the Prophet asked his companions, "Who do you think is the strong man?" The companions replied, "He who can wrestle people down." The Prophet replied, "No, it is he who controls himself when angry." The Prophet also taught us effective anger-management skills: "Anger comes from the Satan; the Satan was created from fire, and fire is extinguished only with water; so when one of you becomes angry, he should perform ritual washing [*wudu*]." And, "When one of you is angry while standing, let him sit down until his anger goes away; if it does not, then let him lie down." Prophet Muhammad encouraged us to be quick in forgiving other people, saying that no two people should stay apart from each other out of anger for more than three days.

17 Arrogance is one of the worst forms of ingratitude and an undignified behavior. Pride removes any sense of shyness before God and before others, and it is a gateway to sin and evil.

And cover not truth with falsehood, nor conceal the truth when you know [what it is].**14**

—QUR'AN 2:42

O you who believe! Persevere, excel in patience, and be constant. Be conscious of God so that you may be successful.**15**

—QUR'AN 3:200

[Righteous are] those who spend generously in times of ease and difficulty, those who control their anger, and those who are forgiving toward people. Surely God loves those who do good.**16**

—QUR'AN 3:134

And swell not your cheek out of pride at men, nor walk in insolence through the earth; for God loves not any arrogant boaster.**17**

—QUR'AN 31:18

How wonderful is the case of a believer; there is good for him in everything and this is not the case with anyone except a believer. If prosperity visits him, he expresses gratitude to God and that is good for him; and if adversity visits him, he endures it patiently and that is better for him.

—PROPHET MUHAMMAD

1 The Arabic word *wassatha*, which I've translated here as "the middle path," can also be translated as "moderate" or "justly balanced."

2 The chief characteristic of a Muslim community, as envisioned by the Qur'an, is one of moderation and balance between theological, ethical, and legal extremes. In the theological realm, Muslim scholars have argued that while Judaism focuses primarily on law and Christianity emphasizes spirituality, Islam finds a middle ground between the two in its teachings on the unity and compatibility of law and spirituality in religion. On the ethical scale, the Qur'an teaches moderation in everything, from eating and drinking (7:31) to spending habits (25:67) to even matters of worship (73:20). In legal matters, the Qur'an strikes a balance between the need for justice and the desire for mercy; for instance, in the matter of retribution it is permissible to seek compensation from an oppressor, but the path of forgiveness is held in higher esteem (42:40–43).

3 "Enjoining what is right" means calling humanity toward all those virtues that are enjoined in scriptural teachings as being qualities of righteous people and societies. Social justice is at the core of this obligation, seeking to uphold the rights of all people, whether rich or poor, man or woman, black or white (Qur'an 4:135). The Qur'an especially emphasizes the good care of orphans (2:220), widows (2:240), disabled people (24:61), and all those who are downtrodden in society (90:12–16). All of these tasks are considered communal obligations (*fard kifaya*), meaning that if a person (or persons) fulfills one of the social needs, then he or she fulfills it on behalf of the entire community; but if no one fulfills a social need, then the whole community is responsible for it individually until the need is fulfilled. "Forbidding what is wrong" means struggling against anything that is considered evil or harmful according to scriptural teachings, such as racism or corrupt business practices. Prophet Muhammad said, "If one of you sees something bad, he should change it with his hand; and if he is not capable of that, then with his tongue; and if he is not capable of that, then with his heart, and that is the weakest form of faith."

11 □ On Envisioning a Just and Moral Society

Thus We have made you a community of the middle path[1] so that you may be witnesses to humanity, and the messenger a witness to you.[2]

—QUR'AN 2:143

You are the best of peoples, evolved for humanity, enjoining what is right, forbidding what is wrong, and believing in God.[3]

—QUR'AN 3:110

The religion of Islam is easy, and whoever makes the religion a rigor, it will overpower him; so follow a middle course. If you cannot do this, do something near to it and give glad tidings and seek divine help in the morning and at dusk and during some part of night.

—PROPHET MUHAMMAD

4 This passage offers a vision for the equality and unity of Muslims in a society where no one is above the law, and everyone is subject to divine laws, rules, and regulations. While these ideals of equality and justice between all members of society are difficult to find nowadays in Muslim and non-Muslim lands, certainly there are many examples of them in early Islamic history that still serve as inspiring models for us today. For example, when the second caliph of Islam, Umar ibn Al-Khattab, traveled from the Islamic capital of Damascus to the conquered land of Jerusalem, he took turns riding and guiding the camel with his servant cameleer. Upon entering the city of Jerusalem it was his turn to guide and the cameleer's turn to ride, so he entered the city on foot while his servant rode. At first the people thought that the servant was the caliph and rushed to greet him until they were informed that the one walking alongside the camel was actually the Caliph Umar. Many other similar stories of the past motivate social reformers in the Muslim world today.

Indeed, this community of yours is one single community, and I am your Lord, so serve Me.**4**

—QUR'AN 21:92

Stand firm [on the straight path] as you are commanded, you and those with you turning to God; and stray not [from the path], for God sees well all that you do.

—QUR'AN 11:112

And [people] have been commanded no more than this: to worship God, offering sincere devotion, being true [in faith]; to establish regular prayer; and to practice regular charity. That is true religion.

—QUR'AN 98:5

5 *Zakat* is a social institution that is meant to help the poor and weak members in society. It is considered a right of poor people over rich Muslims, and consists minimally of 2.5 percent of a person's total wealth. For the rich, it is a way of purification of the soul and of past sins, and a moral lesson in giving out from the gifts of God to those who do not have.

6 Poor is someone who cannot afford even basic living for one day; needy is someone who has enough for a basic living on most days but meets all of his or her expenses with extreme difficulty.

7 Meaning those employed to properly collect and administer the almsgiving, and also those who help poor and weak people in society, such as employees of a soup kitchen.

8 This usually been understood as those who recently converted to Islam and may be facing social hardships due to their decision. Another interpretation is any non-Muslim who is in need of help and is not belligerent toward Muslims.

9 That is, to free slaves, unjust prisoners of war, victims of oppression and tyranny, and so on.

10 As long as this debt has not been accrued by unlawful means, such as gambling.

11 This can take several forms, such as supporting a religious school or building a mosque.

12 This means anyone who is a refugee or anyone who is lost while traveling.

Alms [*zakat*]**5** are only for the poor and needy,**6** and the workers who administer them,**7** and those whose hearts have been reconciled,**8** and those in bondage,**9** and those in debt,**10** and on the cause of God,**11** and for the wayfarer,**12** as an ordinance of God. And God is omniscient, most wise.

—QUR'AN 9:60

Of [people's] goods, take alms, so that you might purify and sanctify them, and pray on their behalf. Verily your prayers are a source of security for them, and God is One who hears and knows [all things].

—QUR'AN 9:103

The best charity is to feed an empty stomach.

—PROPHET MUHAMMAD

Whosoever clothes another Muslim, God will clothe him on the Day of Requital with clothes of paradise.

—PROPHET MUHAMMAD

13 Muslims believe that Islam is a complete way of life that requires surrendering to God's will for those who embrace it as their own. This is the path chosen by God for those who follow the Qur'an and *sunnah*, the way of the Prophet. As such, preservation of religion in a Muslim society is among the foremost goals of Islamic law, which makes the outward religious practices easy and accessible for anyone who chooses to be Muslim. Non-Muslims must be free to practice their own religion without any restrictions or hardships (Qur'an 2:256), and such freedoms must be protected in society (Qur'an 22:39–41). Non-Muslims in Muslim lands are protected peoples (*dhimmi*), allowed to freely practice their religion as long as families pay a protection tax (*jizyah*) to the government (Qur'an 9:29), similar to the obligatory almsgiving (*zakat*) of Muslims. Prophet Muhammad encouraged the proper treatment of *dhimmis,* saying, "Whoever hurts a *dhimmi,* hurts me. And whoever hurts me, annoys God" and "Beware! On the Day of Requital, I shall myself be the complainant against him who wrongs a *dhimmi,* or lays on him a responsibility greater than he can bear, or deprives him of anything that belongs to him." Some historians have criticized the treatment of *dhimmis* in different periods of Islamic history, but they neglect to recognize that the treatment of religious minorities in these periods of history was generally much worse in non-Muslim lands. If anything, Islamic civilization produced some of the most tolerant and religiously pluralistic societies in human history, such as Muslim rule of Spain (711–1492), which Jewish historians refer to as the "Golden Age of Jewry," and during the Ottoman Empire (1299–1922), where minority religions were allowed to form their own communities and courts of civil law. Today, some Muslim nations are better than others in their treatment of religious minorities, but the same can be said of non-Muslim nations as well.

This day have I completed your religion for you, completed My favors upon you, and have chosen for you willful surrender unto God's Will [*islam*] as your religion.[13]

—QUR'AN 5:3

The Prophet was asked, "O Messenger of God, tell me something about Islam which I cannot attain from anyone else." The Prophet replied, "Say, 'I believe in God,' and then remain steadfast."

—PROPHET MUHAMMAD

In the case of those who say, "Our Guardian-Lord is God," and stand straight and steadfast [on the straight path], the angels descend on them [saying]: "Fear you not, nor grieve! Instead receive the glad tidings of the garden, that which you were promised!" We are your protectors in this life and in the hereafter, wherein you shall have all that your soul desires and all that you ask for, a hospitable gift from the Forgiving, the Merciful.

—QUR'AN 41:30–32

14 Every living human soul is sanctified with some portion of divine spirit (Qur'an 32:9) and honored over the rest of creation (Qur'an 17:70). Therefore, killing any innocent human being is completely prohibited, considered the worst sin after associating partners with God (Qur'an 25:68), and equivalent to the killing of all of humanity (Qur'an 5:32). As such, preservation of human life is among the highest purposes of Islamic law.

15 That is, in the execution of a legal sentence, in carrying out a just war, or in individual legitimate self-defense. These exceptions serve as a method of retributive justice and as a deterrent against the most heinous of crimes in society. Penal codes of any type in Islamic law can only be applied by a legitimate political authority, and never by individuals or a group of people acting on their own, for such an act would be equally reprehensible.

16 In the case of an individual murdering another individual, the victim's family has full authority to ask for something other than the death penalty, such as monetary compensation or even clemency (Qur'an 2:178). However, in the case of mass murder, the authority rests with the legal body because such a crime violates moral and social order, and therefore turns into a crime against the state.

17 After a murderer has been punished for his crime, the victim's family has no right to seek additional forms of justice. In all of these laws we can see the Qur'an striking a moral balance between justice for the victims, mercy for the perpetrator, and prevention of cycles of violence.

Nor take life—which God has made sacred[14]—except in the case of justice;[15] And if anyone is slain wrongfully, We have given his heir authority in the matter,[16] but let him not exceed bounds in seeking retribution, for he is aided [by God and law].[17]

—QUR'AN 17:33

A ruler who, having control over the affairs of the Muslims, does not strive diligently for their betterment and does not serve them sincerely, will not enter Paradise with them.

—PROPHET MUHAMMAD

O God, treat harshly those who rule over my community with harshness, and treat gently those who rule over my community with gentleness.

—PROPHET MUHAMMAD

18 The Qur'an encourages people to seek financial independence and livelihood through free trade between communities and across oceans. This enhances the quality of human life and satisfies at least the basic needs for proper living. The Qur'an considers owning property attained by lawful means a sacred right of every individual that must be protected in society. For this reason, stealing is one of the worst social crimes a person can commit and is punished strongly in the Qur'an as a deterrent against such offenses (5:38–39). As such, preservation of property and economy is also one of the primary objectives of Islamic law.

19 Family serves as the foundation of a strong society in Islam. In fact, Muslim scholars equate healthy societies with healthy families, and unhealthy societies with unhealthy families. At its core, a healthy family consists of a husband and wife committed to a relationship of loving-kindness and mercy that translates into a sense of stability and tranquility for the entire family (Qur'an 30:21). At a deeper level, family life is healthy when the rights of everyone within the family are protected and maintained. The hope is that these qualities will then transfer over on a larger scale to produce societies that are stable and tranquil. This is why fornication and adultery—which are chief contributors to the breakdown of the family structure—are considered transgressions against society, and not merely individual transgressions against sacred law. Unlawful sexual relations that are openly displayed in public, that is, witnessed by at least four sound male adults, carry strict social punishments (Qur'an 24:2). However, slandering someone's reputation without proof is equally wrong and punished with similar strictness (24:4). As such, the preservation, protection, and enhancement of families are essential features of Muslim societies.

It is God who has subjected the sea to you, that ships may sail through it by divine command, that you may seek of God's bounty, and that you may be grateful.[18]

—QUR'AN 45:12

O humanity, be conscious of your Guardian-Lord, who created you from one soul, and created its mate from it, and propagated from the two many men and women. And be conscious of God by whom you demand your mutual rights, and of these ties of kinship; for verily God watches over you.[19]

—QUR'AN 4:1

All of you are guardians and are responsible for your wards. The ruler is a guardian and responsible for his subjects; the man is a guardian and responsible for his family; the woman is a guardian and is responsible for her husband's house and his offspring; and so all of you are guardians and are responsible for your wards.

—PROPHET MUHAMMAD

20 This passage constitutes the very first verses revealed by God to Prophet Muhammad in the Qur'an. In it we find an indication of the importance that Islam places on seeking knowledge and wisdom—both religious and otherwise. Prophet Muhammad placed great emphasis on learning: "Seeking knowledge is incumbent upon every Muslim," which *hadith* commentators have understood to be a command for young and old, men and women. The Prophet also spoke of knowledge as a lifelong journey: "Seek knowledge from the cradle to the grave." He also encouraged Muslims to travel far and wide to gain education: "Seek knowledge even if it is as far as China." Sound education is a basic right every child has over his or her parents. Indeed, the hallmark of Islamic civilization, when it was at its peak, was the many contributions of Muslim intellectuals in the fields of mathematics, astronomy, geography, philosophy, and so on. Intellectual discovery across the sciences is deemed essential for the positive growth and dynamism of human society. For this reason, preservation and enhancement of the intellect is considered one of the most important goals of Islamic law. It is a major reason why Islamic law prohibits the consumption of intoxicants, which impair proper reasoning and judgment on a short-term basis and have the potential to permanently damage the brain. Today, many of the problems in the Muslim world are a result of the decline in educational institutions and stagnant intellectual thought. Many Muslim scholars argue that a revival of the Muslim world can only come through a revival of Islam's rich intellectual heritage.

21 Privacy and the protection of human honor and dignity are among the basic rights of every human being, according to Qur'anic teachings. In another place, the Qur'an offers even greater rules and regulations about privacy within the home as a way to maintain dignity even in intimate family settings (24:58–60). In the same spirit, the Qur'an also prohibits and condemns making fun of others, offensive name calling, spying, and backbiting (49:11–12). The idea is that protecting human honor is essential because it leads to the likelihood of people acting in dignified ways and representing themselves honorably within society.

Read, in the name of your Guardian-Lord, Who created: created man out of a clot of congealed blood. Read, for your Guardian-Lord is Most Generous, the One who taught the use of the pen, taught man that which he knew not.[20]

—QUR'AN 96:1–5

O you who believe, enter not houses other than your own, until you have asked permission and greeted with peace those in them; that is best for you, in order that you may be aware [of right conduct]. If you find no one in the house, enter not until permission is given to you. If you are asked to go back, then go back, for that makes for greater purity between yourselves, and God knows well all that you do.[21]

—QUR'AN 24:27–28

Wisdom is the lost treasure of the believer; he seeks it wherever he finds it.

—PROPHET MUHAMMAD

1 According to the Qur'anic worldview, all of humanity shares a common relationship in that all of us can trace our heritage back to a common ancestor in Adam and Eve, who were themselves created from a single soul (*min nafsin wahida*) (Qur'an 4:1). In other places the Qur'an addresses humanity as "Children of Adam" (7:26, for example) to point out this origin we all share, and by which we can truly recognize each other as brothers and sisters. Prophet Muhammad said, "None of you truly believes until he loves for his brother what he loves for himself," and many commentators of that *hadith* emphasize that "brother" in this context refers to all of humanity.

2 It is part of God's plan, design, and will to place us all in different races, nations, and tribes. This way we can come together to marvel at God's creative genius in which we find a multitude of colors, languages, and personalities—all possessing their own unique beauty. And when we recognize that this great diversity of races is God's will, then we come to know and appreciate one another's cultures, beliefs, and practices. The diversity of the human race is not reason or cause for enmity; enmity is an unnatural state that is introduced into the human condition by the whisperer of evil (Qur'an 41:36).

3 Righteous conduct and behavior is what truly sets apart human beings from one another, and not the superficial elements of race, nationality, and class. In the words of civil rights hero Martin Luther King, Jr., we should "not be judged by the color of our skins, but by the content of our character."

12 □ On Pluralism, Inclusive Theology, and Interfaith Relations

O humanity, We created you from a single pair of a male and a female,[1] and made you into races and tribes so that you may come to know each other.[2] Verily the most honored of you in the sight of God is the most God-conscious of you.[3] And God has full knowledge and is well-acquainted of all things.

—QUR'AN 49:13

There are two qualities which you possess that God loves: clemency and tolerance.

—PROPHET MUHAMMAD

God has revealed to me that you should be courteous to one another. One should neither hold himself above another nor transgress against another.

—PROPHET MUHAMMAD

4 | If you reflect on everything that is in the heavens and on earth, the one pattern you will discover is diversity and variation. The sun and the moon, the petals of flowers, the features and capacities of animals—all exhibit a range and multiplicity of color, design, and function. The human species is no different; we, too, are part of God's creation, which is in itself a proof of divine existence, reality, and attributes. To then take this beautiful diversity of God's creation as reason to discriminate and dishonor human beings who do not look and speak like us is unconscionable and can only be attributed to people of extreme ignorance. We all would do well to heed the counsel of Prophet Muhammad during his farewell address, in which he said, "All humanity is from Adam and Eve; an Arab has no superiority over a non-Arab nor a non-Arab any superiority over an Arab; also a white has no superiority over a black nor a black any superiority over white, except by piety and good action."

And among the signs of God is the creation of the heavens and the earth, and the variations in your languages and your colors. Verily in that are signs for those who know.[4]

—QUR'AN 30:22

We have established rites for every community to observe, so do not let them draw you into dispute about the matter; but appeal to God, for you are certainly following guidance that is sound. If they argue with you, then say, "God knows best what you are doing." God will judge among you, on the Day of Resurrection, regarding what you differed on.

—QUR'AN 22:67–69

5 | Muslims believe that all communities on earth at one time or another received noble prophets who taught their people the difference between truth and falsehood, good and evil (Qur'an 35:24). Some of the accounts of these prophets are mentioned in the Qur'an and many of them are not (Qur'an 40:78). But the essential message of all the prophets has always been the same: There is nothing worthy of worship except God, and therefore we must surrender ourselves to God by practicing good and virtuous deeds, which we will be questioned about on the Day of Requital (Qur'an 16:36). What differed between the prophets were particularities in the law, which evolved over time depending on the place and time of a people.

6 | Plurality of religious laws and practices is part of divine will, for if God had wanted, all of us would practice religion in the same exact way. In understanding and embracing this reality there is an understanding and embracing of God's will. For Muslims this does not mean giving up their own truth-claims, but it does mean accepting the fact that not everyone will practice in the same manner and that there is divine wisdom in that.

7 | Instead of arguing, bickering, and plotting against one another, the Qur'an says that it is more beneficial and productive for us to engage in the doing of good deeds. This is the central teaching of all world religions. Muslims involved in interfaith work often look to this verse in particular for inspiration.

To each among you have We prescribed a law and a revealed way.[5] And if God had so willed, God would have made you a single people; but the intent is to test you in what God has given you.[6] Vie, then, with one another in doing good works. The return of you all is to God, Who will then tell you about that wherein you differed.[7]

—QUR'AN 5:48

Speaking kindly to people itself is an act of charity.

—PROPHET MUHAMMAD

8 Since it is part of God's will that not all human beings believe the same thing or practice in the same way, to force someone to believe or practice faith is simply impermissible (Qur'an 10:99). As such, everyone must be free to believe and practice what their own conscience tells them to be true and right. This is why wherever the early Muslims went, they never forced anyone to convert to Islam, but instead protected other houses of worship and allowed the inhabitants of the land to practice their own religion freely. The idea that Islam was spread by the sword—a common belief in Western culture—is an unfortunate and false reading of history. From the onset of Islam, Prophet Muhammad formed what is known as the Constitution of Medina, which stated: "The Jews [of Medina] will be treated as one community with the Believers, and the Jews will have their religion protected." Years later, when the Muslims conquered Jerusalem, Caliph Umar made a covenant with the inhabitants of the land, which in part read, "[Umar] grants to all, whether sick or healthy, security for their lives, their possessions, their churches and their crosses, and for all that concerns their religion. Their churches shall not be changed into dwelling places, nor destroyed, neither shall they or their appurtenances be in any way diminished, nor the crosses of the inhabitants, nor aught of their possessions, nor shall any constraint be put upon them in the matter of their faith, nor shall anyone of them be harmed." The fact that there remains till this day ancient houses of worship from other religions and significant non-Muslim populations in much of the Muslim world is clear evidence of Islam's history of tolerance. Unfortunately, however, such tolerance is not present everywhere in the Muslim world today.

9 Here the Qur'an reaffirms its vision of an inclusive theology whereby the prophets and original revelations of Jews and Christians in particular are accepted and celebrated as being true. There is also reaffirmation of the notion that we all truly worship One God. In another place, the Qur'an actually calls on Jews, Christians, and Muslims to come together on common ground in the essential belief of monotheism (3:64).

Let there be no compulsion in religion. Truth stands out clear from falsehood. Whoever rejects evil and believes in God has grasped the most trustworthy handhold that never breaks. And God hears and knows all things.[8]

—QUR'AN 2:256

And do not argue with People of the Book unless it is in a most kindly manner, except with those of them who have been unjust. Say [to them], "We believe in revelation which has come down to us and in that which came down to you. Our God and your God is One, and it is unto God that we surrender ourselves.[9]

—QUR'AN 29:46

A disagreement occurred between two of the Prophet's companions, Abu Dharr and Bilal, who was a black man from Abyssinia, during the course of which Abu Dharr said: "You son of a black woman." The Messenger of God was extremely upset with Abu Dharr's comment, so he rebuked him by saying, "You still have ignorance remaining within you, O Abu Dharr. He who has a white mother has no superiority over the son of a black mother."

—PROPHET MUHAMMAD

10 In this verse the conditions for attaining sure salvation are summa- rized into three aspects: absolute belief in One God, believing in a day of accountability for the life lived, and the working of righteous deeds on earth. This path of salvation is open to everyone, whether they are Muslim or not. In reality, any who live their lives according to at least these three core teachings are in fact *muslim* in the sense that they have surrendered their will to God. It must be noted, however, that this verse in no way guarantees paradise to Muslims, Jews, Christians, and Sabians (ancient monotheists who lived in Arabia at the time); rather it opens up the possibility of everyone being able to achieve salvation if they do what is necessary to gain it.

11 In order to sanctify and enhance healthy communal relations with Jews and Christians, the Qur'an permits Muslims to engage with Peo- ple of the Book—Jews and Christians—in two essential ways: eating and marriage. Both of these social functions allow for intimate friend- ship and love to develop between people, and provide a means to form genuine community. Eating meat prepared by polytheists and intermar- rying with them is not permissible (though sharing vegetarian meals is permissible), because the meat may have been prepared while invoking a deity other than God, and a sanctified marriage requires at least that both the bride and groom share a common belief in One God.

The Muslims, the Jews, the Christians, and the Sabians—any who believe in One God and the last day and do good deeds have their reward with their Lord. There is nothing for them to fear; they will not sorrow.[10]

—QUR'AN 2:62, 5:69

This day are all things good and pure made lawful for you. The food of the People of the Book is lawful for you and yours is lawful for them; and so are chaste believing women, and chaste women from among People of the Book when you give them their bridal gift, seeking to preserve their chastity, not to prostitute them, and not taking them as secret lovers.[11]

—QUR'AN 5:5

Say: "O People of the Book, come to common terms as between us and you: that we worship none but God; that we associate no partners with God; that we erect not, from among ourselves, lords and patrons other than God." If then they turn back, say you: "Bear witness that we are those who surrender to the will of God."

—QUR'AN 3:64

12   This entire passage was revealed as a clarification to an earlier verse, which states: "O you who believe, take not the Jews and the Christians as patrons, for they are but patrons to each other. And he amongst you that turns to them is of them. Verily God guides not a people unjust" (5:51). Unfortunately this verse is still invoked in radical circles to discourage any type of interfaith relations, and by unfair critics of Islam to promote the false idea that Islam is a religion of intolerance. The reality is that both of these groups have a habit of taking verses (their own scripture and the scripture of others) out of their scriptural and historical contexts to support their own particular agenda. When this verse is read in its scriptural context we find a clarification of its meaning and scope in 60:8–9, which clearly encourages Muslims to practice "loving-kindness and justice" with peaceful non-Muslims and to avoid such close relationships with those non-Muslims who are engaged in killing Muslims and driving them out of their homelands. When we study the historical context of 5:51 we find that this verse was revealed at a time when Jewish and Christian communities in Arabia aided the pagan Arabs in an attack on the Muslim community of Medina. It is in this context that the Qur'an discourages associating and especially seeking political alliance with or protection from Jews and Christians. But as long as any group is peaceful toward the Muslims, Muslims must be peaceful, kind, and just toward them.

God does not forbid with regard to those who do not fight you for your faith nor drive you out of your homes, from dealing in loving-kindness and justice with them, for God loves those who are just. God only forbids you, with regard to those who fight you for your faith, and drive you out of your homes, and support others in driving you out, from turning to them [for friendship and protection]. It is such as turn to them [in these circumstances] that do wrong.[12]

—QUR'AN 60:8–9

He who believes in God and the Last Day must not harm his neighbor, and he who believes in God and the Last Day must show hospitality to his guest, and he who believes in God and the Last Day should speak good or remain silent.

—PROPHET MUHAMMAD

✦ Much has been said and written about Islam's position on peace and war after the tragic events of 9/11, which placed the Islamic tradition under a critical microscope. The reality is that Qur'anic commentaries, both in the classical and modern period, have understood this critical issue in vastly different ways. Interpreters' sociopolitical contexts prove to be essential factors in their articulation of a worldview on peace, war, and reconciliation. What must be said from the outset, though, is that commentators on the Qur'an have never understood the principle of *jihad* to be exclusively or even primarily a concept of war. This is because the linguistic meaning of *jihad* is "to struggle" and has nothing to do with war, conflict, or fighting. Furthermore, the Qur'an uses the word *jihad* (or one of its derivatives) several times to denote a spiritual (29:6, 29:69), theological (25:52), moral (22:78), or financial (9:20) struggle that, again, does not infer fighting in any way. In fact, when the Qur'an does speak exclusively about war, it carefully distinguishes between the principle of *jihad* and the concept of *qital*, which can be translated as "fighting." The popular translation of *jihad* as "holy war" is incorrect (the Arabic equivalent of such a concept would be *harb* (war) *muqadis* (holy)—a term that does not exist in the Qur'an or *hadith*). This chapter attempts to explain the Qur'anic basis for peace, reasons for allowing just war, ethical conduct of war, and teachings on reconciliation through a thorough examination of relevant passages and their scriptural-historical contexts.

1 The individual and communal state that God calls us to in the Qur'an is a state of peace within ourselves (89:27) and between ourselves (49:10). The word for peace in Arabic is *salam,* which comes from the root word *salima,* meaning such things as "sound," "safe," "wholeness," and so on. Interestingly, the word *islam* is born out of the same root, which shows how closely associated the concept of peace is to the central message of the religion.

13 □ On Peace, War, and Reconciliation

And God does call to the abode of peace. God does guide whom God wills to a way that is straight.[1]

—Qur'an 10:25

The believers are a single brotherhood, so make peace and reconciliation between them, and be in awe of God, that you may receive divine mercy.

—Qur'an 49:10

Faith is a restraint against all violence, so let no believer commit violence.

—Prophet Muhammad

A true believer is one with whom others feel safe. One who returns love for hatred.

—Prophet Muhammad

2   At the heart of individual and social peace is the concept of justice and equity (*adl*). At the individual level, justice and equity mean giving the intellect, soul, and body their due rights, depriving none of its essential needs. For instance, completely depriving the body of food causes disturbance to the intellect and soul and in turn causes you to be in a perturbed state. Similarly, at the social level, justice and equity mean providing all social functions their appropriate rights in order to meet the essential needs of members in a society. For example, if a society uses most of its wealth to build a strong army while neglecting educational institutions, then it will cause a major imbalance. Interestingly, the Qur'an regards disobedience toward God as an act of oppression against a person's own soul (39:53). So as much as this passage forbids us from oppressing another created being, it is also an admonition about the way we treat ourselves. In the Islamic tradition it is widely understood that the best way to prevent shameful deeds—stealing, taking drugs, prostitution, and so on—is to exercise justice in all its forms and to avoid oppression in all its forms, for doing so will eliminate many of the root causes associated with such actions. When justice is present, it dismantles the causes of oppression, which in turn leads to a state of peaceful harmony within the individual and within the society.

3   In order for the ideals of peace to work, justice must be given the highest priority in a society, because one injustice leads to another injustice and the cycle of disharmony continues. To achieve peace, the patterns of injustice need to be broken and replaced with more equitable and fair patterns that are beneficial to all members of society and hold all members of society to a common standard. What most often takes us away from the ideal principles and practices of justice is our own desire to place ourselves and those we like above the law and rule of justice. When this happens, and especially when this becomes prominent within a society, the entire society disintegrates into a tribal mentality, with warring groups, factions, and classes preferring their own preservation and growth over any sense of order or justice. For this reason, the Qur'an requires us to stand up firmly for the cause of justice even if it is against our own self-interest, for in this manner we will be contributing positively to the ultimate goal of peace.

God commands justice, the doing of good, and giving to others; and God forbids all shameful deeds, injustice, and oppression. God instructs you so that you may be mindful.[2]

—QUR'AN 16:90

O you who believe, stand out firmly for justice, as witnesses to God, even against yourselves, or your parents, or your siblings, and whether it be against rich or poor, for God can best protect both. Follow not your lusts, lest you swerve, and if you distort or decline to do justice, verily God is all acquainted with all that you do.[3]

—QUR'AN 4:135

Be on your guard against committing oppression, for oppression will be darkness on the Day of Resurrection; and be on your guard against stinginess because it doomed those who were before you, it incited them to shed blood and treat the unlawful as lawful.

—PROPHET MUHAMMAD

4 In the Qur'anic worldview, enmity and hatred between individuals and groups of people are seen as unnatural and undesirable in the human condition. Therefore, it is said that enmity is introduced into the human condition through the whisperer of evil, Satan, who uses many different means to incite ill will, jealousy, hatred, and so on. This is partly why, when you enter a gathering of any kind, it is encouraged that you quietly seek refuge in God from Satan (Qur'an 41:36, 114) and openly greet those around you with "Peace be upon you" (*Assalamu' alaykum* in Arabic)—in order to ward off anything that may lead to hostility between yourself and others (Qur'an 4:86).

O you who believe, stand out firmly for God, as witnesses to fairness, and let not the hatred of others cause you to swerve toward wrong and depart from justice. Be just, that is closer to piety, and be conscious of God, for God is well-acquainted with all that you do.

—QUR'AN 5:8

Satan's plan is to excite enmity and hatred between you.[4]

—QUR'AN 5:91

In most secret talk there is no good, unless [such secret talk] exhorts to a deed of charity or justice or conciliation between people, for the one who does this, seeking the good pleasure of God, We shall soon give the highest reward.

—QUR'AN 4:114

5   Jealousy and other spiritual diseases of the heart can create such a disruption in our consciousness that we end up losing the peaceful element of our being and are then vulnerable to committing reprehensible acts of hostility. An understanding of the self is essential in understanding the root causes of war and conflict.

6   Prophet Muhammad taught us that "Toward the latter days of indiscriminate violence, be like the first and better of the two sons of Adam who said, 'If you raise your hand to kill me, I will not raise mine to kill you. Surely I fear God, the Lord of the worlds.'" Indeed, the righteous son of Adam serves as a role model for the highest ethical and moral standards that we as individuals can display in an era of dangerous modern technology (such as cluster bombs and nuclear weapons) that has made violence and killing tragically indiscriminate. It is only in the practice of self-restraint, like the son of Adam, that we break cycles of violence.

7   Despite the glorification of violence and killing in most human societies and during most periods of history, the reality is that such actions lead to tragedy not only for the victims, but also for the perpetrators of the crime, who must live their lives with an enormous sense of guilt.

8   The value of human life is immeasurable, for once a life is lost it can never be replaced. As such, the Qur'an likens the murder of one innocent person to the murder of all humanity, and the saving of one innocent person to the saving of all humanity. Murder is among the worst crimes and sins that can be committed between human beings (Qur'an 25:68).

Recite to them the truth of the story of the two sons of Adam. Behold, they each presented a sacrifice to God, which was accepted from one, but not from the other.[5] Said the latter, "Be sure I will slay you." "Surely," said the former, "God does accept the sacrifice of those who are righteous. If you do stretch your hand against me, to slay me, it is not for me to stretch my hand against you to slay you, for I do fear God, the Cherisher of the worlds. For me, I intend to let you draw on yourself my sin as well as your own, for you will be among the companions of the fire, and that is the reward of those who do wrong."[6] The soul of the other led him to the murder of his brother; he murdered him, and became one of the lost ones. Then God sent a raven, who scratched the ground to show him how to hide the shame of his brother. "Woe is me!" said he, "was I not even able to be as this raven, and to hide the shame of my brother?" Then he became full of regrets.[7] On that account We ordained to the Children of Israel that if anyone killed a person— unless it be for murder or for spreading mischief in the land—it would be as if he killed all of humanity; and if anyone saved a life it would be as if he saved the life of all humanity.[8] Then although there came to them Our messengers with clear signs, yet, even after that, many of them continued to commit excess in the land.

—QUR'AN 5:27–32

9 Here the Qur'an recounts the story of Bilquis, a famous Queen of the vast empire of Sheba, and the wisdom she exhibits in deciding not to invade Prophet Solomon's kingdom despite the counsel she receives from the warmongers. Bilquis wisely says that when armies go into a land seeking to exploit its resources and oppress its people, the natural result is turmoil, anarchy, and corruption in the land; and when this happens even the noblest of people in that land become miserable and hopeless, leading them to commit dishonorable acts and engage in shameful behavior. Many commentators of the Qur'an have understood this passage as God's denunciation of all political might gained through brutal violence for the sake of exploitation, because such actions inevitably lead to subjugation, misery, and moral chaos.

10 In remaining true to the position that peace can only be achieved by elevating justice and eliminating oppression, the Qur'an permits the limited use of physical force in defeating forces of injustice and tyranny. The argument goes as follows: There are evil, tyrannical, oppressive people and forces on earth who seek to dominate the world and spread their mischief throughout the lands. To face this reality, God allows for courageous people to stand up against such armies in order to stop their oppression and to replace their evil with what is good. If God did not allow people to fight against evil, then the forces of evil would be free to rule the earth. The illustration for this argument is given in the story of Prophet David, who was able to defeat Goliath against all odds and put an end to Goliath's reign of tyranny. It is on this premise that the Qur'an permits fighting in certain situations with certain conditions. From the onset, though, it is made clear that such fighting is permissible only for the sake of justice and repelling harm. It is not for the purpose of land, glory, or exploitation.

[In response to King Solomon's letter, the Queen of Sheba] said, "O chiefs, advise me in my affair, for no affair have I decided except in your presence." They said, "We are endued with strength, and given to vehement war, but the command is with you, so consider carefully what you will command." She said, "Kings, when they enter a country, corrupt it, and turn the noblest of its people into the most abject. And this is the way they always behave. But I am going to send a gift to them and await whatever the ambassadors bring back."[9]

—QUR'AN 27:32–35

When [Talut and his army] advanced to meet Goliath and his forces, they prayed, "Our Lord, pour out patience on us and make our steps firm. Help us against those who reject faith." By God's will they routed them, and David slew Goliath, and God gave [David] power and wisdom and taught him whatever God willed. And did not God check one set of people by means of another, the earth would indeed be full of mischief, but God is full of bounty to all the worlds.[10]

—QUR'AN 2:250–251

11 This entire passage is the first set of verses revealed in the Qur'an giving Muslims permission to fight in self-defense, according to Qur'anic commentators. Historically, it must be pointed out that the Muslims were a persecuted minority in the land of Mecca during the first thirteen years of Prophet Muhammad's prophetic life. During this period, even though Muslims were tortured and killed by the pagan Arabs, they were not allowed to fight even in self-defense and were commanded to be patient in the face of hardship. Then, when Prophet Muhammad and his community of believers migrated to the land of Medina and established themselves as a community there at the invitation of its people, they were given the permission, and even the obligation, to defend the community against the hostile forces that sought to destroy them. Therefore, the Qur'an specifically states that permission to fight is only granted to those who have been wronged, affirming the universal right of self-defense.

12 Another situation in which the Qur'an allows Muslims to fight is in defense of houses of worship and for the universal freedom to practice religion. Here the permission to fight is justified on the premise that had fighting been absolutely prohibited, those forces that would like to destroy houses of worship and eliminate religion from the world would prevail on earth.

13 Permission to fight under certain circumstances is not meant to contribute to cycles of violence or the tendency for the oppressed to become oppressors. Rather, fighting can only be used as a means for elevating justice and ending cycles of violence and revenge. This is why the Qur'an describes true warriors of God as those who, when given victory on earth, maintain a strict spiritual discipline of prayer, give charity to the poor and needy, and strive to spread goodness and prevent evil. Anything short of this cannot be considered a just war, nor can it be considered a struggle that God supports.

To those against whom war is made, permission is given [to fight], because they have been wronged, and verily God is Most Powerful for their aid.[11] They are those who have been expelled from their homes against all rights for no other reason except that they say, "Our Lord is God." Did not God check one set of people by means of another, surely monasteries, churches, synagogues, and mosques, in which the name of God is commemorated abundantly, would have been destroyed.[12] God will certainly aid those who aid divine cause, for verily God is full of Strength, Exalted in Might. And they are those who, if We establish them in the land, remain constant in prayer and give regular charity, enjoin the right, and forbid the wrong.[13] And with God rests the outcome of all affairs.

—QUR'AN 22:39–41

14 Here again the principle of self-defense is invoked as a permissible justification for fighting, but with the clearly stated stipulation that such fighting must occur within strict moral and ethical boundaries. To know what these boundaries are, Muslim scholars look to the practice of Prophet Muhammad and the first four rightly guided caliphs who succeeded him in leadership. Probably the best summary of ethical guidelines concerning the conduct of war in Islam is found in a saying of the first noble caliph, Abu Bakr, when his army set out for Syria, which was still part of the Byzantine Empire at the time: "Stop, O people, so that I may give you ten rules for your guidance in the battlefield. Do not commit treachery or deviate from the right path. You must not mutilate dead bodies. Neither kill a child, nor a woman, nor an aged man. Bring no harm to the trees, nor burn them with fire, especially those which are fruitful. Slay not any of the enemy's flock, except for your food. You are likely to pass by people who have devoted their lives to religion, so leave them alone." The Qur'an also includes in its ethical teachings of war a prohibition against forced conversions (2:256), breaking of oaths and treaties (16:91–92), arrogance or mischief in victory (28:83), and a command toward the humane treatment of prisoners of war (8:70, 47:4) and giving protection to anyone who seeks it (9:6). In these teachings, which are confirmed by numerous prophetic sayings, Muslims are commanded to conduct themselves according to the highest ethical standards that take into account not only human life, but also all other life.

15 This verse within the passage is often taken out of scriptural context to mean anyone who is not a believer. However, the earlier verse clearly contextualizes this verse with "those who fight you," which simply does not apply to just anyone. This verse also articulates an essential Qur'anic worldview that "Oppression is even worse than killing." The idea is that killing an innocent human being is cruel and unjustified, but in death a person at least finds an end to his or her suffering, whereas oppression causes unending suffering, psychological disturbance, and moral chaos that in the end are even worse than killing. As such, fighting to eliminate oppression is justified even if it involves taking the life of oppressors.

Fight in the cause of God those who fight you, but do not transgress limits, for God loves not transgressors.[14]

—QUR'AN 2:190

And slay [those who fight you] wherever you come upon them, and turn them out from where they have turned you out, for oppression is even worse than killing.[15] But fight them not at the Sacred Mosque, unless they first fight you there; but if they fight you, slay them, for such is the recompense of those who suppress faith. But if they cease, God is Oft-Forgiving, Most Merciful.

—QUR'AN 2:191–192

God will torment those who torment people in this world.

—PROPHET MUHAMMAD

16 The objectives of permissible fighting are reinforced and summarized as three: first, to eliminate oppression in all of its forms; second, to elevate justice in all of its ways (also see Qur'an 8:39); and third, for the freedom to believe in God and act accordingly. Sometimes this third objective is misunderstood to mean that those who do not believe in God should be fought, and that fighting should continue until they believe in God. However, this would contradict the clear and well-established Qur'anic principle, "Let there be no compulsion in religion" (2:256). As such, this third objective simply means that Muslims can fight for the freedom and preservation of religion.

17 Despite the noble aims and objectives set out in the Qur'an for fighting against oppression, fighting must cease if those who initiated the fighting stop and mend their ways, even if the objectives are not met, because the preferred state of affairs between people is always peace. This is why the Qur'an says in another place, "And if the enemy inclines toward peace, you too incline toward peace, and trust in God, for God hears and knows all things. Should [the enemy] intend to deceive you, verily God suffices you, for it is God that has strengthened you with divine aid and with the believers" (8:61–62).

18 True warriors of God are those who respond to the cry of the oppressed, not those who themselves oppress or go to war seeking wealth and glory, and certainly not those who transgress the due limits and boundaries of war (Qur'an 2:190).

19 It would be simpleminded of us to look at the category of "believers" and "those who reject faith" as identifiable groups of people rather than qualitative or moral categories of people. This passage and several of those above clearly indicate that the "believer" is someone who seeks justice and the end of oppression. Anything short of this does not truly represent the "believer," nor does it represent "the cause of God."

And fight [those who fight you] until there is no more oppression, and there prevails justice and faith in God;**16** but if they cease, let there be no hostility except to those who practice oppression.**17**

—QUR'AN 2:193

And why should you not fight in the cause of God and of those who, being weak, are oppressed—men, women, and children whose cry is, "Our Lord! Rescue us from this town whose people are oppressors, and raise for us from Yourself one who will protect, and raise for us from Yourself one who will help!"**18** Those who believe fight in the cause of God, and those who reject faith fight in the cause of evil.**19** So fight you against the friends of Satan, feeble indeed is the cunning of Satan.

—QUR'AN 4:75–76

20 This verse has been termed the Verse of the Sword by radical interpreters of the Qur'an who argue that this verse "abrogates" other
more tolerant and humane verses on fighting. However, upon exam-
ining the scriptural and historical context of the verse, it is hard not to
believe that this argument for "holy war" was concocted as an attempt
to justify radical notions of *jihad* by certain individuals, groups, and
governments. If we read verses 9:1–4, the verses preceding 9:5, the
first thing that becomes clear is that the context surrounding this passage is one in which the Qur'an is responding to a break in the peace
treaty between the pagan Arabs and the Muslim community. In fact,
9:4 even offers an exception to the limited context of the passage by
saying, "Treaties are not dissolved with those pagans with whom you
have entered into alliance and who have not subsequently failed you in
any way, nor aided anyone against you. So, fulfill your treaties with
them to the end of their term, for God loves the God-conscious." Furthermore, if we look at verse 9:6, the verse after the so-called Verse
of the Sword, it offers an important qualification: "If one amongst the
pagans seek you for asylum, grant it to him, so that he may hear the
Word of God; and then escort him to where he can be secure. That is
because they are men without knowledge." As such, we can conclude
that this entire passage was revealed with reasons and qualifications
in response to a specific event in which a peace treaty was broken. So
it can very well be argued that this entire passage can be categorized as
time- and place-bound (*khass*), rather than general or universal (*'aam*)
in its application.

21 The Qur'an says that we must always be open to the possibility of
reconciliation, whether between individuals or societies, and even to
consider the possibility of enmity turning into love by the grace of God.
In times of war and conflict, the ultimate goal of peace must never be
lost. And peace can never be achieved if we are unable to imagine
friendship and love with our "enemies." Therefore, the first step
toward reconciliation is the courage to imagine, hope, and dream that
one day things will be different.

But when the forbidden months are past, then fight and slay the pagans wherever you find them, and seize them, beleaguer them, and lie in wait for them in every place; but if they repent, and establish regular prayers and practice regular charity, then open the way for them, for God is Oft-Forgiving, Most Merciful.[20]

—QUR'AN 9:5

It may be that God will grant love between you and those whom you hold as enemies, for God has power over all things, and God is Oft-Forgiving, Most Merciful.[21]

—QUR'AN 60:7

My servants, I have made injustice forbidden to myself, and I have made it forbidden to you, so do not be unjust.

—DIVINE SAYING RELATED BY PROPHET MUHAMMAD

22 | The Qur'an recognizes the value of justice and in making right the wrongs of the past in order to reach a position of reconciliation. Therefore, it is permissible for victims of injustice to seek just retribution. However, the higher moral position is with the person who chooses forgiveness and reconciliation over his or her right to justice, because such a course facilitates the path to peace, which is the ultimate goal of all reconciliation projects.

23 | What is unacceptable is for a victim of injustice to seek out more in retribution than what he or she was made to suffer, and to use the victim mentality and position to unleash oppression on others. Here the Qur'an, in its teachings on reconciliation, is attempting to break the common historical pattern of the oppressed becoming oppressors, and victims of evil turning into perpetrators of evil.

24 | At the heart of the Qur'anic prescription for reconciliation is the principle of forgiveness even when we are angry, because forgiveness has a powerful healing quality. Forgiveness liberates the soul from the burden of anger, and it is an absolute requirement in mending relationships. Therefore, the next step in reconciliation, after opening the door to its possibility, is actually going out and seeking forgiveness from each other, and overcoming the feelings of anger.

25 | The most beautiful way for reconciliation to occur is by warding off and getting rid of the ill feelings and mistrust that have built up over time. This can be done by doing something good and kind for the person, group, or nation with whom you are attempting reconciliation. The exchanging of gifts, charitable acts, and kindness helps replace bad memories and ill feelings with good thoughts and warm feelings. In this way, the path to reconciliation is paved, and the possibility for converting hatred into intimate friendship becomes real.

The recompense for an injury is an injury equal thereto [in degree]; but if a person forgives and makes reconciliation, his reward is due from God, for God loves not those who do wrong.[22] But indeed if any do help and defend themselves after a wrong has been committed against them, there is no blame against such a person. The blame is only against those who oppress men and commit wrongdoing and insolently transgress beyond bounds through the land, defying right and justice, for such there will be a penalty grievous.[23] But indeed if any show patience and forgive, that would truly be an exercise of courageous will and resolution in the conduct of affairs.[24]

—QUR'AN 42:40–43

For good and evil are not equal: Promote what is better, and then one between you and whom there was enmity will become like intimate friends.[25] But no one will be granted such goodness except those who exercise patience and self-restraint, none but persons of the greatest good fortune. So if an incitement to discord is made to you by the Evil One, seek refuge in God, for God hears and knows all things.

—QUR'AN 41:34–36

1 Qur'anic stories are meant to guide us in the ways of good conduct with God and fellow human beings. These stories also ultimately shape our worldview—the way we think about the universe and the characters it is made of. The first prominent story featuring women is the account of Adam and Eve, the parents of humanity. Here Eve, representing the primordial woman, lives with Adam on equal footing, enjoys the same delights from God's blessings, and is expected to follow the same divine commandments. In other passages, both Adam and Eve are said to be created from a single soul (*min nafsin wahida*) (4:1, 7:189). Equality of men and women as spiritual beings is emphasized from the outset.

2 In transgressing the sacred law, Adam and Eve are both tempted by Satan and consequently fall into sin together. Eve is not depicted as a temptress, nor does she aid the devil against Adam (man). Both immediately become aware of the consequences of sin and are remorseful for their actions. As such, men and women equally possess the ability to obey God and to transgress against divine law. The whisperer of such transgression is Satan, not the woman Eve.

3 Adam and Eve, upon spiritual awakening and realization, turn to God in repentance, acknowledging their shortcomings and seeking divine guidance. God turns to both of them in mercy and forgiveness and reveals to them the ways of guidance (Qur'an 2:37–38). Thus, women have the spiritual and moral capacity, like men, to return to God after sin, and God returns equally to all who seek forgiveness.

4 Adam and Eve experience the consequence of sin by falling out of the blissful state of paradise and into the instability of worldly life; however, neither is made to bear more in consequences than the other, unlike the punishments Eve is given in the biblical account (Genesis 3:16). In the Qur'anic account, God rewards and punishes men and women with equal measure and justice.

14 □ On Women and Gender Relations

O Adam, dwell in the garden, you and your wife, and eat of whatever you two want; but do not approach this tree, for then you would be transgressors.[1] Then Satan whispered to the two, to reveal to them their private parts, which had been concealed from them: "Your Guardian-Lord only prohibited you from this tree lest you two become angels, or you become immortals." And he swore to them: "I am a sincere advisor to you." Thus he led them by false hopes: then when they tasted of the tree, their private parts became evident to them and they began to sew together leaves from the garden over themselves.[2] Then their Guardian-Lord called to them, "Did I not forbid you from that tree, and tell you Satan is an open enemy to you?" The couple said, "Our Guardian-Lord, we have wronged our own selves. If you do not forgive us and have mercy on us, we will certainly be among the lost ones."[3] God said, "Become you enemies, some unto another; you will still have a place to live on earth, and provisions for a while." God said, "There you will live, and there you will die, but you will be raised back to life."[4]

—QUR'AN 7:19–25

A believer must not harbor any rancor against a believing woman; if he dislikes one of her characteristics he will be pleased with another.

—PROPHET MUHAMMAD

5 This story highlights the virtue and greatness of Hagar, mother of Abraham's firstborn son, Ishmael. A similar account of Hagar can be found in Genesis 21, but with a few key differences that further inspire Muslim spirituality in general, and women's spirituality in particular. We see that in the Islamic narrative, Hagar possesses a remarkable trust in and reliance on God when she accepts Abraham's decision to abandon her and Ishmael in the barren desert, understanding that Abraham is acting out of divine command. Hagar simply, yet profoundly, declares: "I am satisfied with God." Instantly, Hagar becomes the spiritual voice for oppressed and abandoned people everywhere.

6 In the biblical account Hagar sits and weeps under a tree after Abraham abandons her until an angel of hope appears with good news. In the Islamic tradition, Hagar is depicted as a courageous seeker who refuses to sit back and just wait for fate; she believes and trusts in God but knows that she must work and struggle to receive divine aid. When Muslims visit the House of God in Mecca, one of the rites they perform is a reenactment of Hagar's footsteps in which they walk hurriedly between the same two mountains of Marwa and Safa to celebrate her teaching to humanity: If we sincerely desire change in our condition, we must trust in God and then set out to achieve the changes we seek.

7 Hagar's courage and struggle for change gave birth to a whole new civilization that would eventually witness the birth of one of the greatest human beings, Prophet Muhammad, centuries later.

When Abraham and his wife [Sarah] had the differences they had, he set out with Ishmael and Ishmael's mother with a water skin, containing some water. Ishmael's mother began to drink from the water skin and suckled her child until they reached Mecca where [Abraham] placed [Hagar] under a large tree. Then Abraham left to return to his family. Ishmael's mother followed him until they reached Kada', when she called out behind him, "O Abraham! With whom are you leaving us?" He said, "With God." She said, "I am satisfied with God,"[5] and she went back and began to drink from the water skin and nurse her child until the water was finished. She said, "If I go and look perhaps I will find someone." She went and climbed Safa and looked and looked to see whether she could find someone, but she did not see anyone. When she reached the valley, she ran to the top of Marwa. She did that several times. Then she said, "I should go and see what is happening with the child." She went and looked and there he was in the same condition as if he was gasping at the brink of death. She could not contain herself and said, "If I go and look perhaps I will find someone." She went and climbed Safa and looked and looked but did not see anyone, until she had done that seven times.[6] Then she had just said, "I should go and look and see what is happening with him," when she heard a voice. She said, "Help me, if You possess any good!" Then the angel Gabriel appeared and dug his heel into the earth and water began to spring forth. Ishmael's mother was astonished and began to dig.[7]

—PROPHET MUHAMMAD

8 The story of the mother of Moses draws many parallels to the story of Hagar in that it is a tale of great trust and reliance on God for the sake of a beloved child. Here we also see a woman with the spiritual capacity to receive words of divine inspiration, like the male prophets were given. Perhaps what inspires both Hagar and the mother of Moses to rely so perfectly on God and to perform acts of great courage is the divine-like mercy and compassion they had for their children, which by its very nature drew them closer in station to God, whose pre-eminent attributes are the Merciful and the Compassionate. In fact, in all of these stories, compassion seems to be an innate characteristic of the female.

9 Pharaoh's wife, known as Asiyya in the Islamic tradition, was a pious woman of great compassion who tactfully struggled against the tyrannical ways of her husband. Here she is shown playing a major role in saving the life of Moses, who would otherwise have been killed as part of Pharaoh's mandate to murder all Hebrew male infants. For this reason, the Qur'an elevates Asiyya to the position of a role model for all those who oppose tyranny (66:11). Thus, Asiyya is an antithesis of the stereotypical depiction of women as weak and fearful; in Asiyya we truly find a model of bravery and courage.

10 These are the concluding lines to a longer story on the wisdom and spiritual depth of the Queen of Sheba, known as Bilquis in the Islamic tradition, who demonstrates sound judgment in not going to war with Solomon's kingdom (27:32–34) and in surrendering herself to God upon hearing the prophetic words of Solomon. Bilquis demonstrates wisdom and good leadership, which is a powerful model to look for in an age of unwise leadership in the world. For Muslim women it is also a story of inspiration as to the effective role they can play in leadership capacities if they exercise the same kind of intelligence and discretion in decision making as Bilquis.

And We inspired the mother of Moses, "Nurse him, but when you fear for him, cast him into the river and don't be afraid or aggrieved, for We will restore him to you, and We will make him a messenger."**8** Then Pharaoh's people took him in, to be an opponent and a sorrow to them; for Pharaoh, Haman, and their troops were sinners. The wife of Pharaoh said, "This is a joy for me and for you; do not kill him. Perhaps he may be useful to us or we may adopt him as a son."**9** And they were not aware. But the heart of the mother of Moses came to be desolate; she almost revealed who he was, and would have had We not strengthened her heart, so she would be one of the faithful. So she said to his sister, "Trail him." So she watched him from a distance, unbeknownst to them. And We forbade him the breast at first; so then she said, "Shall I show you people of a house who will feed him for you, and be counselors to him?" Thus We returned him to his mother, that she might be glad and not grieve, and that she know the promise of God is true; and yet most of them are unaware.

—QUR'AN 28:7–13

[Queen of Sheba said]: "O my Guardian-Lord, I have indeed wronged my own soul; I do willingly surrender, with Solomon, to the Guardian-Lord of the Worlds."**10**

—QUR'AN 27:44

11 Mary is one of the most honored and revered figures in the Islamic tradition. There is an entire chapter (*surah* 19) in the Qur'an that is named "Mary." She is described as a role model for all of humanity (Qur'an 3:42, 66:12). Mary was a woman who was devoted entirely to God, and she would even seclude herself from the family for days as she dedicated herself to spiritual purification and elevation (Qur'an 3:37, 43). For us all, and for Muslim women in particular, Mary's story is meant to inspire a life of service and devotion to God and the purification of the soul as a way of drawing near to God.

12 One of the most praiseworthy aspects of Mary's life was the modesty she practiced in front of men and the chastity she maintained as an unmarried woman. Islam teaches that the hidden physical beauty of both men and women is something so sacred that it must only be shared with an intimate spouse and companion. Mary is the highest example of this modesty and chastity, and therefore elevated as a role model for Muslim men as much as for women.

13 Here Mary's story parallels those of Hagar and the mother of Moses in that she is put through an enormous ordeal, but her trust in God bears fruit in divine providence. Her childbirth is described as painful, but one for which there are many spiritual blessings and rewards. This imagery speaks generally also to the many different types of hardships we may face in our lives, and how trusting in God and patience will see us through in the end, elevating us to a higher station with God, just as God elevated Mary to an honored position over the rest of humanity.

And mention Mary in the Book when she withdrew from her people to a place in the East, and secluded herself from them, We sent her Our spirit, which appeared to her just like a man.[11] She said, "I take refuge from you with the Benevolent One if you are God-conscious." He said, "I am only a messenger from your Guardian-Lord, to give you a sinless son." She said, "How will I have a son, when no man has touched me and I have not been unchaste?"[12] He said, "It will be so." He said, "Your Guardian-Lord says, 'It is easy for Me; and We intend to make him a sign for humankind, and a mercy from Us.' So the matter is decided." So she carried him, secluding herself with him in a faraway place. Then labor pains impelled her to the trunk of a palm tree. She said, "Would that I had died before this and been completely forgotten!" Then a voice called to her from below, saying, "Do not grieve; your Guardian-Lord has put a stream beneath you, and shake the trunk of the palm tree toward you to let fresh ripe dates fall by you. Then eat and drink and be of good cheer: but if you see any man, say, 'I have dedicated a fast to the Benevolent One, so I shall not speak to any human being today.'"[13]

—QUR'AN 19:16–26

14 Among the greatest role models for Muslim women are the stories of the wives of Prophet Muhammad, who are endearingly referred to as "Mothers of the Believers" (*Umm al-Mu'mineen*). These thirteen women, married to the Prophet at various times during his life, ranged from young to old, virgin to widow, black skinned to white skinned, intellectual and scholarly to witty and humorous, wise and powerful to simple and humble. These noble women played major roles in society during the Prophet's lifetime and after his death. In fact, the Prophet's first wife, Khadija, was a rich and influential businesswoman who had employed Muhammad and then proposed marriage to him after being impressed with his honesty and integrity. Later, Khadija would be the first one to assure the Prophet that the revelation he experienced from God was true, and was the first to follow the Prophet into Islam. Another wife, Umm Salama, served as one of the Prophet's political advisors, offering him wise counsel during the Treaty of Hudabiyyah, which was a peace contracted between all the warring parties of Arabia. Ayesha, often referred to as the most beloved of the Prophet's wives, became a great scholar after the Prophet's death and was responsible for narrating nearly one-third of the authentic *hadith* literature we have available to us today. The caliphs who succeeded Prophet Muhammad always sought Ayesha's counsel on religious, social, and political issues of the day. Ayesha even led an army during one of the controversial civil wars that ensued shortly after the Prophet's death. These are just three brief accounts of the virtuous and powerful lives of the Mothers of the Believers, whose lives and sayings are studied with much admiration in the Islamic sciences. To this day these women serve as model wives, scholars, activists, and leaders for Muslim women and men.

The Prophet is closer to the believers than their own selves, and his wives are their mothers.[14]

—QUR'AN 33:6

Show reverence to the Messenger of God by honoring the members of his family.

—SAYING OF COMPANION ABU BAKR

The Messenger of God drew four lines on the ground, then he said to his companions, "Do you know what this is?" [The companions] said, "God and the Messenger of God know best." The Messenger of God said: "The best of the women of paradise are Khadijah bint Khuwaylid [the Prophet's first wife], Fatimah bint Muhammad [the Prophet's beloved daughter], Aasiya bint Mazaahim the wife of Pharaoh [who protected Moses as an infant], and Maryam bint 'Imran [the mother of Jesus], may God be pleased with them."

—PROPHET MUHAMMAD

15 Islam was probably the earliest civilization to grant women full inheritance rights and ownership of property rights that in no way could be
compromised after marriage. Up until the twentieth century men
would inherit their wives' wealth and property in the West, but Islam
prohibited such practices from its very beginnings in the seventh century. While it is true that women usually receive about half of what
their male counterpart receives in the divisions of inheritance (Qur'an
4:11–12), it is also true that women have no legal obligation to spend
their money on anyone else, while men have a legal obligation to
financially care for their wives, children, parents, unmarried siblings,
and even more under certain circumstances in Islamic law. As such,
men receiving double inheritance to women is a means of facilitating
their role in the family, and not a way to prefer them over females. It
is no surprise then that many women in Islamic civilization accumulated
so much wealth that they were able to endow some of the best institutions of learning in the Muslim World, such as the Al-Qarawiyyin
Mosque and University in Morocco, founded by Fatima Al-Fihri in 859
C.E. Financial independence for women is encouraged and facilitated
in the sacred law of Islam, and it has the potential to be resurrected
for the empowerment of women today.

16 This passage summarizes the entire Qur'anic worldview of women in
relation to men: They possess equal capacity for noble qualities and
piety; they are expected to have and are held responsible for developing the same praiseworthy characteristics within themselves; and they
are equal in the sight of God, having been promised equal divine forgiveness and reward for all that they do in the way of goodness. Several other passages underscore the same teaching (40:40, 16:97, for
example). Interestingly, this verse was revealed in response to a woman
in Prophet Muhammad's community who asked why all the verses
revealed were directed toward men. This and other verses were
revealed to make it clear that the Qur'an is indeed addressing all of
humanity—women and men alike—and calls everyone to the same
qualities and virtues.

Men are to have a portion of what is left by their parents and closest kin; and women are also to have a portion of what is left by their parents and closest kin—an assigned portion of whatever there is of it, be it a little or a lot.[15]

—QUR'AN 4:7

For the men who willingly surrender to the will of God, and the women who willingly surrender to the will of God; the men who believe and the women who believe, the men who are devout and the women who are devout, the men who are truthful and the women who are truthful, the men who are constant and the women who are constant, the men who are humble and the women who are humble, the men who give charity and the women who give charity, the men who fast and the women who fast, the men who are chaste and the women who are chaste, and the men and women who remember God abundantly, God has arranged forgiveness for them, and a magnificent reward.[16]

—QUR'AN 33:35

17 The Arabic word *awliyah* comes from the root word *wali* meaning "protecting benefactor," "helper," "ally," "successor," "heir," or "guardian." Another associated root word is *waliya*—to be close or near. Given the context of this passage, I have merged the two root words to translate *awliyah* as "close helpers," which is nearer to its comprehensive meaning. Other translators usually go with just "protectors" or "friends." Regardless of the word we choose, this term establishes a very close and mutually respectful relationship between men and women.

18 In terms of gender relations, the Qur'an envisions a positive, healthy, and beneficial relationship that is oriented toward a greater goal and purpose. This passage clearly encourages women to participate in the moral, social, and political construction of society in which the ultimate aim is to promote and spread all that is beneficial for people, and to divert and prevent all that is harmful for people. Muslim women who engage in social and political activism often draw inspiration from this passage. For these women, rights to sociopolitical participation are not a modern feminist ideology that they struggle with; rather, they are part and parcel of the divinely enjoined directives they find for themselves in scripture.

The believing men and believing women are close helpers[17] of each other; they enjoin what is good and forbid what is evil, and practice prayer and give charity, and obey God and God's messenger.[18] They are the ones on whom God will have mercy. For God is almighty, most wise. God has promised the believing males and the believing females gardens beneath which rivers flow to abide in them, and pleasant dwellings in gardens of eternity. But approval from God is greater; that is the most important success.

—QUR'AN 9:71–72

The world and all things in the world are precious, but the most precious of all in the world is [the company of] a virtuous woman.

—PROPHET MUHAMMAD

And their Lord answered them, "I am never unmindful of the work of a worker among you, male or female. You are from each other."

—QUR'AN 3:195

19 Modesty is often associated primarily or solely with women. However, the Qur'an teaches us that modesty—in terms of clothing, behavior, and gender interaction—is as much a duty of men as it is of women. The purpose of modesty is to preserve and enhance the innate dignity that we all possess by virtue of our being human (Qur'an 17:70), and to see each other through this prism of honor and respect. Modesty engenders pure, innocent, and healthy interaction between the genders and discourages disrespectful behavior, such as sexual impropriety, from occurring. In another passage, the Qur'an offers particular reasons for women's modesty, saying that it wards off unwanted advances from unruly men in society (34:59). "Lower their eyes" simply means not to stare lustfully at the opposite sex, and instead to avert the eyes to maintain purity and respect for each other. As such, it is actually considered more respectful in Muslim cultures not to stare at someone of the opposite sex, while looking people in the face when talking to them is considered respectful in Western culture. Similarly, out of this sense of modesty, it is more proper in Muslim culture not to shake hands or hug between genders.

Tell the believing men to lower their eyes and guard their chastity. That is more pure for them; for God is fully aware of whatever they do.[19]

—QUR'AN 24:30

Once the Prophet came upon several young men who were occupying the road and asked, "Why do you sit along the paths? Avoid sitting in the paths of people." They replied: "There is no harm in our sitting as we only sit and discuss [matters of] knowledge." The Prophet said, "If you must sit, you should fulfill the rights of the path: Do not stare at people, respond to salutations of peace, and talk in a manner that is good."

—PROPHET MUHAMMAD

A man must not look at a man's private parts nor must a woman look at a woman's private parts; neither should two men lie under one cover, nor should two women lie under the same cover.

—PROPHET MUHAMMAD

20 "Not to show their ornaments" has been interpreted as the natural beauty women possess and the added beauty in the way of accessories. "Except the obvious ones" has been interpreted in traditional commentaries as a woman's face, hands, and feet—and sometimes even less, for example just the eyes—based on the Prophet's teachings to the women around him. More modernist interpretations understand this to mean whatever is normally or decently left uncovered in the existing times and cultures.

21 The Arabic word *khimar* is a type of head covering that was worn by honorable upper-class women even before the advent of Islam in Arabia and other places. The Qur'an extends this tradition to all Muslim women—who deserve the same respect as upper-class women—by maintaining the head covering and elongating it over the neck and chest in order to foster greater modesty. This way of dressing mirrors the modest covering of Mary, the mother of Jesus, which can be seen even in modern-day paintings and depictions, and is similar to the modest clothing of Orthodox Jewish women and nuns in the Catholic tradition.

22 The Arabic word *furooj* has been translated in many different ways, but given the context of the passage, I think the most accurate term is "allure," because what women are being discouraged from in this verse is purposefully being sensual or flirtatious with other men.

23 All of these exceptions take into account the private conduct of a woman in her own home and with members of her own household. Privately both men and women have more leeway in the way they dress and in their conduct.

And tell the believing women to lower their eyes and guard their chastity, and not to show their ornaments except the obvious ones,[20] and to draw their head coverings over their bosoms[21] and not to show their allure[22] except to their husbands, or their fathers, or their husbands' father, or their sons, or their husbands' sons, or their brothers, or their brothers' sons, or their sisters' sons, or their women, or those in bondage to them, or male attendants who are beyond all sexual desire, or very young children who are yet not aware of the nakedness of women.[23] And they should not drum their feet to make known the ornaments they conceal. And turn to God together, O believers, so that you may be happy.

—QUR'AN 24:31

O Children of Adam, We have bestowed clothing on you to cover your private parts, and for adornment. But the garment of piety is best. That is among the signs of God, so they may take a lesson.

—QUR'AN 7:26

1 The companionship of marriage between a man and a woman is the highest form of relationship in the created world because of the unique intimate nature of the marital bond. The desired outcome of this relationship is spiritual and physical tranquility and harmony (*sakeena* in Arabic) for both husband and wife. The teaching here is that both couples should do their best to create this special union for each other and for themselves.

2 One of the primary functions of marriage is to produce offspring in order to positively contribute to the next generation—"be fruitful and multiply" (Genesis 9:1). Leaving behind a virtuous child in the world is considered a continued act of charity that will benefit your soul till the end of time (*sadaqa jarriyyah*), according to Prophet Muhammad. As such, couples should see the raising of good children to be one of the highest acts of cooperation between men and women that the Qur'an speaks so fondly of (9:71).

3 Commentators of Qur'an say that in this verse we find the two keys to a happy marriage: loving affection (*mawadah*) and merciful compassion (*rahmah*). Loving affection means to treat your spouse with utmost kindness and fairness; to prefer your spouse's needs and wishes over your own; and to satisfy your spouse's physical and spiritual need for intimacy and friendship. Merciful compassion means always being there to comfort your spouse in times of emotional need; covering your spouse's faults and shortcomings in front of other people; forgiving and overlooking mistakes that your spouse makes to a reasonable degree; and focusing on the good aspects of your spouse's behavior and personality, rather than on the weaker ones. In another passage, the Qur'an describes the ideal relationship between husband and wife with the likeness of garments (2:187) that offer comfort, protection, privacy, and beauty for each other. When a marital relationship is built in this way and with this sort of foundation, the inevitable result is tranquility, safety, and comfort (*sakeena*) for the whole family.

15 □ On Marriage and Family Life

God it is who created you all from a single soul, making its mate from it, to dwell in tranquility with her.[1] Then when they have mated, she bears a light burden, and goes about with it. Then when she becomes heavy, they both pray to God, their Guardian-Lord: "If you give us a healthy child, we will certainly be grateful."[2]

—QUR'AN 7:189

And among the signs of God is having created mates for you from yourselves that you may dwell in tranquility with them, creating loving affection and merciful compassion between you.[3] Surely there are signs in that for people who reflect.

—QUR'AN 30:21

[Servants of the Merciful are] those who pray, "Our Guardian-Lord, grant us delight in our spouses and children and make us foremost among the God-conscientious." They will be rewarded with the highest of heavenly abodes for their constancy, and they will be greeted there with salutations and peace, to remain there forever, an excellent dwelling place and abode.

—QUR'AN 25:74–76

4 This passage is the one used to prove the acceptability of polygyny (the practice of having more than one wife), which is limited to four in Islamic law. However, there must be absolute fairness between all four wives—economically, spiritually, and physically. If a husband cannot maintain this strict fairness, then Islamic law only allows for one wife. As indicated in this verse, the permissibility of polygyny was historically granted after a major battle left many Muslim women in the Prophet's community widowed or orphaned. It was a way to alleviate this crisis in the community. However, polygyny became a general permissibility and was generally left unchallenged by jurists of Islamic law until the modern period, as some jurists controversially opine that polygyny is only permitted under dire circumstances, such as the one the Prophet's community faced and that some war-torn communities face today in the world. This position is somewhat strengthened by the Qur'an when it seems to discourage the practice by saying: "You will never be able to treat women the same, no matter how hard you try" (4:129). However, all jurists would agree that fairness between the wives is a precondition and that any woman has the right to refuse to be in such a relationship by making such a stipulation in her marriage contract. Polygyny is quite rare today in most Muslim countries, but remains somewhat common in the Gulf region of the Arabian Peninsula. Polyandry (the practice of having more than one husband), on the other hand, is forbidden in Islamic law for many different reasons, the most notable of which is that it would be near impossible, or at least quite difficult, to know who the father is if the woman were to become pregnant. This problem would undermine one of Islamic law's most basic priorities and purposes—preservation of lineage—and would then further complicate things in terms of inheritance rights of the children, which is another important concern in Islamic law.

Give orphans their property, without exchanging bad for good; and do not consume their property commingled with your own, for that is a serious sin. And if you fear you cannot do justice by the orphans, then marry women who please you—two, three, or four—but if you fear you won't be equitable, then only one, or a legitimate bondmaid of yours. That way it is easier for you not to go wrong.[4]

—QUR'AN 4:3

A woman is generally sought as a wife for her wealth, beauty, nobility, or piety; but choose a woman for her piety and you will be happy.

—PROPHET MUHAMMAD

When someone with whose piety and character you are satisfied asks to marry your daughter, comply with his request. If you do not do so, there will be great corruption and great evil on earth.

—PROPHET MUHAMMAD

[5] This passage is a basic directive on the laws of sexual relations between husband and wife. It is clarified in the prophetic teachings that this verse means that only intercourse is unlawful during a woman's menstrual cycle, because it can cause her unnecessary pain and hardship. Other forms of intimacy are permitted and even encouraged during this time.

[6] The Qur'an is using decent language and metaphors to say that a husband and wife may engage in sexual intercourse using more than one position, unlike certain other religious teachings that regulate such intimacy to the "missionary position." However, in all circumstances sexual relations must meet the needs of both husband and wife and take into account the sensitivities of both partners in order to make it an act of human compassion and love, rather than animalistic drive. The Prophet said to his companions, "Do not approach your wife like an animal. Rather, send a messenger to her." They asked, "What is the messenger?" He replied, "Kissing and kind words." Female sexuality is as much a concern to jurists of Islamic law as male sexuality, even though the latter is emphasized more often. In fact, some jurists even maintain that a man is not permitted to leave his wife unfulfilled for more than four days unless there are exceptional circumstances.

[7] Sexual intimacy between husband and wife is as much a spiritual act as a physical one. For this reason, a couple is encouraged to perform some devotional acts of worship before becoming intimate, such as making a joint supplication for a good marriage and righteous offspring. The following supplication is particularly encouraged: "In the name of God, O God, turn Satan from me, and turn Satan from what You bestow upon us."

They also ask you about menstruation. Say, "It hurts, so leave women alone during their period, and do not approach them until they are clean.[5] Then when they have washed themselves, you may come to them any way God has directed you. For God loves those who turn in repentance, and loves those who keep clean." Your wives are a field of yours; so come to your field as you wish,[6] but do something for the good of your souls beforehand. And be conscious of God, and know that you are going to meet God. And give good tidings to the believers.[7]

—QUR'AN 2:222–223

The believers who show the most perfect faith are those who have the best behavior, and the best of you are those who are the best to their wives.

—PROPHET MUHAMMAD

If a woman dies in a state that her husband is pleased with her, she will enter paradise.

—PROPHET MUHAMMAD

8 Here the Qur'an condemns female infanticide, a common pre-Islamic practice among Arab pagans, because the birth of a daughter was considered a shameful curse in certain tribes. Unfortunately this practice continues in some parts of the world where men are preferred over women in society. The Qur'an calls this an evil choice and considers it one of the worst crimes and sins a person can commit (81:8–9). In fact, Prophet Muhammad teaches us that daughters are a source of good news and must be honored: "Whosoever supports two righteous daughters until they mature, he and I will be together like this on the Day of Requital (and he pointed with his two fingers held together to indicate closeness)."

9 This passage highlights the most essential teachings that parents can give to their children through the voice of a wise sage named Luqman. The passage begins by praising the devotion and character of Luqman before it delves into the advice he bestows on his son, which is indicative of the fact that parents must themselves first become the people they desire their children to be because it is in their footsteps that children will most likely follow. Becoming a parent takes enormous strength, wisdom, and patience, all qualities that need to be acquired through devotion to God and commitment to self-purification.

10 The basis of all moral teaching in Islam is a belief in and devotion to the One God, recognizing that there is nothing else worthy of worship except God. Therefore, parents must teach children that fulfilling religious duties, developing noble character, and participating in good deeds should be the highest priorities in their lives, as loving devotees of God.

11 Then children must be cultured into showing gratitude, respect, and compassion toward parents, and especially into honoring the mother. Surely filial piety is the noblest of noble deeds. Only when children are gracious toward their parents can they be gracious toward other human beings.

When one of you is given news of the birth of a female, his face darkens and he grieves within: he hides himself from the people out of distress at the news he's given; shall he keep it, in spite of ignominy, or shall he bury it in the dust? Oh, what an evil decision they make![8]

—QUR'AN 16:58–59

We gave Luqman the wisdom to be grateful to God; and whoever is thankful gives thanks for the benefit of his own soul. And if anyone is ungrateful, well, God is free of all needs, worthy of all praise.[9] Remember how Luqman said to his son, advising him, "My son, don't associate anything with God, for idolatry is a tremendous error."[10] We have entrusted man with care of his parents: his mother bore him, sapped and weakened, and his weaning takes two years: so be grateful to Me, and to your parents. The journey is to Me. If the two of them strive to have you associate what you have no knowledge of with Me, then do not obey them. But keep company with them courteously in this world, and follow the path of those who turn to Me: then it is to Me that you will return, and I will inform you of what you have been doing.[11]

—QUR'AN 31:12–15

12 Children should then be given moral lessons on awareness of divine presence in every instance of their lives, and God's knowledge of all that they do and do not do. Such teachings develop in us an inner conscience (*taqwa*) of what God enjoins and prohibits throughout each day so that we may become stronger in goodness and firmer in warding off sin.

13 The spiritual practice of prayer and meditation seeks to develop a magnanimous soul that carries righteous qualities—such as patience, compassion, and courage—that are beneficial for the self of a child and those around him or her. This also includes teaching children to have an awareness of the social ills confronting their world and what they can do to make this world a better place. In other words, instilling a sense of great purpose in children is essential. And in doing so children need to learn patience and constancy, and the ability to solve and overcome challenges and obstacles that inevitably lie in the path of great goodness.

14 Last, but certainly not least, children must learn good and proper manners and behavior before God and in front of fellow creations. The most essential of good manners are humbleness, gentleness, and moderation, as well as avoiding arrogance, extravagance, and rude behavior.

15 This passage speaks to the marriage counselor or to a friend who would like to help heal a marriage in crisis. Reconciliation between couples is always best and most preferred. But Islam is a practical religion and makes room for worst-case scenarios. In general, divorce is permissible in Islam, but considered a last resort. In the words of the Prophet, "Divorce is the most hated permissible act in the sight of God." Basically, in a husband-initiated divorce, divorce has to be clearly pronounced on three separate occasions between menstrual periods with no sexual relations taking place in between. If sexual relations occur or a couple reconciles during this period, then the marriage resumes. If, however, there is no reconciliation during the time period allotted, then it is considered an irrevocable divorce, which means that the marriage becomes completely void. The Qur'an makes divorce difficult so that it is not done in the heat of the moment, but rather after careful, thoughtful deliberation (2:224–237).

My son, be there the weight of a mustard seed, even be it in rock, or in the skies, or in the earth, God will bring it forth. For God is most subtle, thoroughly aware.[12] My son, pray regularly, enjoin what is fair and forbid the unacceptable. And be constant no matter what happens to you; for that is of the resolve that determines affairs.[13] And don't be contemptuous toward people, and don't swagger around on earth, for God loves no pompous braggart. And moderate your stride, and lower your voice, for the most repulsive sound is surely the braying of an ass.[14]

—QUR'AN 30:16–19

And if you fear a rift between [a husband and wife], then delegate an arbiter from his family and an arbiter from her family. If the two wish to reconcile, God will reconcile them. For God is Knowing, Aware.[15]

—QUR'AN 4:35

Acknowledgments

I would like to thank Maura Shaw for introducing me to Skylight Paths Publishing and encouraging me to write this book. Equal gratitude goes to my brilliant project editor Mark Ogilbee for his invaluable insight and advice on every chapter in this book. I am indebted to Mark for his kindness, patience, and support during every step of the process.

I am truly grateful to Dr. Jane Smith, one of most celebrated professors of Islamic Studies in the United States, for writing the Foreword. I am honored to be her student at the Hartford Seminary and am delighted with her outstanding contribution to this book.

I must also express my deepest appreciation to Dr. Ingrid Mattson for being such a wise teacher and counselor during the last few years. Her vast knowledge of the Islamic sciences and ability to teach the Islamic tradition is a reflection of her illuminated heart, beautiful character, and deep intellect. Much of what I have been able to articulate in this book is a result of what I learned from Dr. Mattson.

Finally, I owe a great deal to my family for their loving care, especially my parents, Talat and Amra, for teaching me how to live, for sharing their love of faith with me, and for being the perfect role models in life.

Notes

Introduction

1. T. C. Young, "The Cultural Contribution of Islam to Christendom," *The Impact of the Arabs and Islam in the European Renaissance,* 1987. (Journal published by the Egyptian National Division of Education, Science and Culture, Cairo.)

2. Karen Armstrong, interviewed on *Religion & Ethics Newsweekly*, PBS, September 13, 2002.

3. Thomas Cleary, *The Essential Koran: The Heart of Islam* (New York: Castle Books, 1993), vii.

A Note on Translation

4. Muhammad Asad, *The Message of the Qur'an* (Gibraltar, Spain: Dar al-Andalus, 1980).

5. Thomas Cleary, *The Qur'an: A New Translation* (Chicago: Starlatch Press, 2004).

Suggestions for Further Reading

Ayoub, Mahmoud. *The Qur'an and Its Interpreters: Volume I*. Albany: State University of New York Press, 1984.

Cleary, Thomas. *The Essential Koran*. Edison, NJ: Castle Books, 1993.

Eaton, Gai. *Islam and the Destiny of Man*. Kuala Lumpur, Malaysia: The Islamic Texts Society, 1994.

Gamard, Ibrahim. *Rumi and Islam: Selections from His Stories, Poems, and Discourses—Annotated and Explained*. Woodstock, VT: SkyLight Paths Publishing, 2004.

Haleem, Muhammad. *Understanding the Qur'an: Themes and Styles*. New York: I. B. Tauris Publishers, 2001.

Murad, Khurram. *Way to the Qur'an*. Leicester, UK: The Islamic Foundation, 1992.

Nasr, Seyyed. *The Heart of Islam: Enduring Values for Humanity*. New York: HarperCollins, 2002.

Omar, Abdul Mannan. *The Dictionary of the Holy Qur'an*. Hockessin, DE: NOOR Foundation, 2003.

Sultan, Sohaib. *The Koran for Dummies*. Hoboken, NJ: Wiley Publishing, 2004.

Mazrui, al-Amin 'Ali. *The Content of Character: Ethical Sayings of the Prophet Muhammad*. Translated by Hamza Yusuf. London: Sandala LLC, 2005.

AVAILABLE FROM BETTER BOOKSTORES.
TRY YOUR BOOKSTORE FIRST.

Global Spiritual Perspectives

Spiritual Perspectives on America's Role as Superpower
by the Editors at SkyLight Paths

Are we the world's good neighbor or a global bully? From a spiritual perspective, what are America's responsibilities as the only remaining superpower? Contributors:
Dr. Beatrice Bruteau • Dr. Joan Brown Campbell • Tony Campolo • Rev. Forrest Church • Lama Surya Das • Matthew Fox • Kabir Helminski • Thich Nhat Hanh • Eboo Patel • Abbot M. Basil Pennington, ocso • Dennis Prager • Rosemary Radford Ruether • Wayne Teasdale • Rev. William McD. Tully • Rabbi Arthur Waskow • John Wilson
5½ x 8½, 256 pp, Quality PB, 978-1-893361-81-2 **$16.95**

Spiritual Perspectives on Globalization, 2nd Edition
Making Sense of Economic and Cultural Upheaval
by Ira Rifkin; Foreword by Dr. David Little, Harvard Divinity School

What is globalization? Surveys the religious landscape. Includes a new Discussion Guide designed for group use.
5½ x 8½, 256 pp, Quality PB, 978-1-59473-045-0 **$16.99**

Hinduism / Vedanta

The Four Yogas
A Guide to the Spiritual Paths of Action, Devotion, Meditation and Knowledge
by Swami Adiswarananda 6 x 9, 320 pp, HC, 978-1-59473-143-3 **$29.99**

Meditation & Its Practices
A Definitive Guide to Techniques and Traditions of Meditation in Yoga and Vedanta
by Swami Adiswarananda 6 x 9, 504 pp, Quality PB, 978-1-59473-105-1 **$19.99**

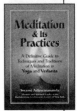

The Spiritual Quest and the Way of Yoga: The Goal, the Journey and the Milestones
by Swami Adiswarananda 6 x 9, 288 pp, HC, 978-1-59473-113-6 **$29.99**

Sri Ramakrishna, the Face of Silence
by Swami Nikhilananda and Dhan Gopal Mukerji
Edited with an Introduction by Swami Adiswarananda; Foreword by Dhan Gopal Mukerji II
Classic biographies present the life and thought of Sri Ramakrishna.
6 x 9, 352 pp, HC, 978-1-59473-115-0 **$29.99**

Sri Sarada Devi, The Holy Mother
Her Teachings and Conversations
Translated with Notes by Swami Nikhilananda; Edited with an Introduction by Swami Adiswarananda
6 x 9, 288 pp, HC, 978-1-59473-070-2 **$29.99**

The Vedanta Way to Peace and Happiness by Swami Adiswarananda
6 x 9, 240 pp, HC, 978-1-59473-034-4 **$29.99**

Vivekananda, World Teacher: His Teachings on the Spiritual Unity of Humankind
Edited and with an Introduction by Swami Adiswarananda
6 x 9, 272 pp, Quality PB, 978-1-59473-210-2 **$21.99**

Sikhism

The First Sikh Spiritual Master
Timeless Wisdom from the Life and Teachings of Guru Nanak by Harish Dhillon
Tells the story of a unique spiritual leader who showed a gentle, peaceful path to God-realization while highlighting Guru Nanak's quest for tolerance and compassion. 6 x 9, 192 pp, Quality PB, 978-1-59473-209-6 **$16.99**

Or phone, fax, mail or e-mail to: SKYLIGHT PATHS Publishing
Sunset Farm Offices, Route 4 • P.O. Box 237 • Woodstock, Vermont 05091
Tel: (802) 457-4000 • Fax: (802) 457-4004 • www.skylightpaths.com
Credit card orders: (800) 962-4544 (8:30AM–5:30PM ET Monday–Friday)
Generous discounts on quantity orders. SATISFACTION GUARANTEED. Prices subject to change.

Children's Spirituality

ENDORSED BY CATHOLIC, PROTESTANT, JEWISH, AND BUDDHIST RELIGIOUS LEADERS

Remembering My Grandparent: A Kid's Own Grief Workbook in the Christian Tradition *by Nechama Liss-Levinson, PhD, and Rev. Molly Phinney Baskette, MDiv*
8 x 10, 48 pp, 2-color text, HC, 978-1-59473-212-6 **$16.99** *For ages 7–13*

Does God Ever Sleep? *by Joan Sauro, CSJ; Full-color photos*
A charming nighttime reminder that God is always present in our lives.
10 x 8½, 32 pp, Quality PB, Full-color photos, 978-1-59473-110-5 **$8.99** *For ages 3–6*

Does God Forgive Me? *by August Gold; Full-color photos by Diane Hardy Waller*
Gently shows how God forgives all that we do if we are truly sorry.
10 x 8½, 32 pp, Quality PB, Full-color photos, 978-1-59473-142-6 **$8.99** *For ages 3–6*

God Said Amen *by Sandy Eisenberg Sasso; Full-color illus. by Avi Katz*
A warm and inspiring tale of two kingdoms that shows us that we need only reach out to each other to find the answers to our prayers.
9 x 12, 32 pp, HC, Full-color illus., 978-1-58023-080-3 **$16.95**
For ages 4 & up (a Jewish Lights book)

How Does God Listen? *by Kay Lindahl; Full-color photos by Cynthia Maloney*
How do we know when God is listening to us? Children will find the answers to these questions as they engage their senses while the story unfolds, learning how God listens in the wind, waves, clouds, hot chocolate, perfume, our tears and our laughter.
10 x 8½, 32 pp, Quality PB, Full-color photos, 978-1-59473-084-9 **$8.99** *For ages 3–6*

In God's Hands *by Lawrence Kushner and Gary Schmidt; Full-color illus. by Matthew J. Baeck*
9 x 12, 32 pp, Full-color illus., HC, 978-1-58023-224-1 **$16.99** *For ages 5 & up (a Jewish Lights book)*

In God's Name *by Sandy Eisenberg Sasso; Full-color illus. by Phoebe Stone*
Like an ancient myth in its poetic text and vibrant illustrations, this award-winning modern fable about the search for God's name celebrates the diversity and, at the same time, the unity of all the people of the world.
9 x 12, 32 pp, HC, Full-color illus., 978-1-879045-26-2 **$16.99**
For ages 4 & up (a Jewish Lights book)

Also available in Spanish: **El nombre de Dios**
9 x 12, 32 pp, HC, Full-color illus., 978-1-893361-63-8 **$16.95**

In Our Image: God's First Creatures
by Nancy Sohn Swartz; Full-color illus. by Melanie Hall
A playful new twist on the Genesis story—from the perspective of the animals. Celebrates the interconnectedness of nature and the harmony of all living things. 9 x 12, 32 pp, HC, Full-color illus., 978-1-879045-99-6 **$16.95**
For ages 4 & up (a Jewish Lights book)

Noah's Wife: The Story of Naamah
by Sandy Eisenberg Sasso; Full-color illus. by Bethanne Andersen
This new story, based on an ancient text, opens readers' religious imaginations to new ideas about the well-known story of the Flood. When God tells Noah to bring the animals of the world onto the ark, God also calls on Naamah, Noah's wife, to save each plant on Earth.
9 x 12, 32 pp, HC, Full-color illus., 978-1-58023-134-3 **$16.95**
For ages 4 & up (a Jewish Lights book)

Also available: **Naamah:** Noah's Wife (A Board Book)
by Sandy Eisenberg Sasso; Full-color illus. by Bethanne Andersen
5 x 5, 24 pp, Board Book, Full-color illus., 978-1-893361-56-0 **$7.99** *For ages 0–4*

Where Does God Live? *by August Gold and Matthew J. Perlman*
Using simple, everyday examples that children can relate to, this colorful book helps young readers develop a personal understanding of God.
10 x 8½, 32 pp, Quality PB, Full-color photo illus., 978-1-893361-39-3 **$8.99** *For ages 3–6*

Children's Spirituality—Board Books

Adam and Eve's New Day (A Board Book)
by Sandy Eisenberg Sasso; Full-color illus. by Joani Keller Rothenberg
A lesson in hope for every child who has worried about what comes next.
Abridged from *Adam and Eve's First Sunset*.
5 x 5, 24 pp, Full-color illus., Board Book, 978-1-59473-205-8 **$7.99** *For ages 0–4*

How Did the Animals Help God? (A Board Book)
by Nancy Sohn Swartz; Full-color illus. by Melanie Hall
Abridged from *In Our Image*, God asks all of nature to offer gifts to humankind—
with a promise that they will care for creation in return.
5 x 5, 24 pp, Board Book, Full-color illus., 978-1-59473-044-3 **$7.99** *For ages 0–4*

Where Is God? (A Board Book) *by Lawrence and Karen Kushner; Full-color illus. by*
Dawn W. Majewski A gentle way for young children to explore how God is with
us every day, in every way. Abridged from *Because Nothing Looks Like God*.
5 x 5, 24 pp, Board Book, Full-color illus., 978-1-893361-17-1 **$7.99** *For ages 0–4*

What Does God Look Like? (A Board Book)
by Lawrence and Karen Kushner; Full-color illus. by Dawn W. Majewski
A simple way for young children to explore the ways that we "see" God. Abridged
from *Because Nothing Looks Like God*.
5 x 5, 24 pp, Board Book, Full-color illus., 978-1-893361-23-2 **$7.95** *For ages 0–4*

How Does God Make Things Happen? (A Board Book)
by Lawrence and Karen Kushner; Full-color illus. by Dawn W. Majewski
A charming invitation for young children to explore how God makes things happen in
our world. Abridged from *Because Nothing Looks Like God*.
5 x 5, 24 pp, Board Book, Full-color illus., 978-1-893361-24-9 **$7.95** *For ages 0–4*

What Is God's Name? (A Board Book)
by Sandy Eisenberg Sasso; Full-color illus. by Phoebe Stone
Everyone and everything in the world has a name. What is God's name?
Abridged from the award-winning *In God's Name*.
5 x 5, 24 pp, Board Book, Full-color illus., 978-1-893361-10-2 **$7.99** *For ages 0–4*

What You Will See Inside ...

This important new series of books, each with many full-color photos, is
designed to show children ages 6 and up the Who, What, When, Where, Why
and How of traditional houses of worship, liturgical celebrations, and rituals of
different world faiths, empowering them to respect and understand their own
religious traditions—and those of their friends and neighbors.

What You Will See Inside a Catholic Church
by Reverend Michael Keane; Foreword by Robert J. Keeley, EdD
Full-color photos by Aaron Pepis
8½ x 10½, 32 pp, Full-color photos, HC, 978-1-893361-54-6 **$17.95**

Also available in Spanish: **Lo que se puede ver dentro de una iglesia católica**
8½ x 10½, 32 pp, Full-color photos, HC, 978-1-893361-66-9 **$16.95**

What You Will See Inside a Hindu Temple
by Dr. Mahendra Jani and Dr. Vandana Jani; Full-color photos by Neirah Bhargava and Vijay Dave
8½ x 10½, 32 pp, Full-color photos, HC, 978-1-59473-116-7 **$17.99**

What You Will See Inside a Mosque
by Aisha Karen Khan; Full-color photos by Aaron Pepis
8½ x 10½, 32 pp, Full-color photos, HC, 978-1-893361-60-7 **$16.95**

What You Will See Inside a Synagogue
by Rabbi Lawrence A. Hoffman and Dr. Ron Wolfson; Full-color photos by Bill Aron
8½ x 10½, 32 pp, Full-color photos, HC, 978-1-59473-012-2 **$17.99**

Children's Spiritual Biography

MULTICULTURAL, NONDENOMINATIONAL, NONSECTARIAN

Ten Amazing People
And How They Changed the World
by Maura D. Shaw; Foreword by Dr. Robert Coles
Full-color illus. by Stephen Marchesi

For ages 7 & up

Black Elk • Dorothy Day • Malcolm X • Mahatma Gandhi • Martin Luther King, Jr. • Mother Teresa • Janusz Korczak • Desmond Tutu • Thich Nhat Hanh • Albert Schweitzer

This vivid, inspirational and authoritative book will open new possibilities for children by telling the stories of how ten of the past century's greatest leaders changed the world in important ways.

8½ x 11, 48 pp, HC, Full-color illus., 978-1-893361-47-8 **$17.95**
For ages 7 & up

Spiritual Biographies for Young People—For ages 7 and up

 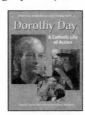 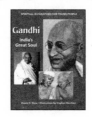 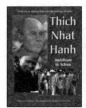

Black Elk: Native American Man of Spirit
by Maura D. Shaw; Full-color illus. by Stephen Marchesi
Through historically accurate illustrations and photos, inspiring age-appropriate activities and Black Elk's own words, this colorful biography introduces children to a remarkable person who ensured that the traditions and beliefs of his people would not be forgotten.
6¾ x 8¾, 32 pp, HC, Full-color and b/w illus., 978-1-59473-043-6 **$12.99**

Dorothy Day: A Catholic Life of Action
by Maura D. Shaw; Full-color illus. by Stephen Marchesi
Introduces children to one of the most inspiring women of the twentieth century, a down-to-earth spiritual leader who saw the presence of God in every person she met. Includes practical activities, a timeline and a list of important words to know.
6¾ x 8¾, 32 pp, HC, Full-color illus., 978-1-59473-011-5 **$12.99**

Gandhi: India's Great Soul
by Maura D. Shaw; Full-color illus. by Stephen Marchesi
There are a number of biographies of Gandhi written for young readers, but this is the only one that balances a simple text with illustrations, photographs, and activities that encourage children and adults to talk about how to make changes happen without violence. Introduces children to important concepts of freedom, equality and justice among people of all backgrounds and religions.
6¾ x 8¾, 32 pp, HC, Full-color illus., 978-1-893361-91-1 **$12.95**

Thich Nhat Hanh: Buddhism in Action
by Maura D. Shaw; Full-color illus. by Stephen Marchesi
Warm illustrations, photos, age-appropriate activities and Thich Nhat Hanh's own poems introduce a great man to children in a way they can understand and enjoy. Includes a list of important Buddhist words to know.
6¾ x 8¾, 32 pp, HC, Full-color illus., 978-1-893361-87-4 **$12.95**

Spirituality

Jewish Spirituality: A Brief Introduction for Christians   *by Lawrence Kushner*
5½ x 8½, 112 pp, Quality PB, 978-1-58023-150-3 **$12.95** *(a Jewish Lights book)*

Journeys of Simplicity: Traveling Light with Thomas Merton, Bashō, Edward Abbey,
Annie Dillard & Others   *by Philip Harnden* 5 x 7¼, 128 pp, HC, 978-1-893361-76-8 **$16.95**

Keeping Spiritual Balance As We Grow Older: More than 65 Creative Ways to
Use Purpose, Prayer, and the Power of Spirit to Build a Meaningful Retirement
by Molly and Bernie Srode 8 x 8, 224 pp, Quality PB, 978-1-59473-042-9 **$16.99**

The Monks of Mount Athos: A Western Monk's Extraordinary Spiritual Journey on
Eastern Holy Ground *by M. Basil Pennington, ocso; Foreword by Archimandrite Dionysios*
6 x 9, 256 pp, 10+ b/w line drawings, Quality PB, 978-1-893361-78-2 **$18.95**

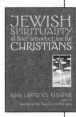

One God Clapping: The Spiritual Path of a Zen Rabbi *by Alan Lew with Sherrill Jaffe*
5½ x 8½, 336 pp, Quality PB, 978-1-58023-115-2 **$16.95** *(a Jewish Lights book)*

Prayer for People Who Think Too Much: A Guide to Everyday, Anywhere Prayer
from the World's Faith Traditions *by Mitch Finley*
5½ x 8½, 224 pp, Quality PB, 978-1-893361-21-8 **$16.99**; HC, 978-1-893361-00-3 **$21.95**

Show Me Your Way: The Complete Guide to Exploring Interfaith Spiritual Direction
by Howard A. Addison 5½ x 8½, 240 pp, Quality PB, 978-1-893361-41-6 **$16.95**

Spirituality 101: The Indispensable Guide to Keeping—or Finding—Your Spiritual Life
on Campus *by Harriet L. Schwartz, with contributions from college students at nearly thirty
campuses across the United States* 6 x 9, 272 pp, Quality PB, 978-1-59473-000-9 **$16.99**

Spiritually Incorrect: Finding God in All the Wrong Places *by Dan Wakefield; Illus. by
Marian DelVecchio* 5½ x 8½, 192 pp, b/w illus., Quality PB, 978-1-59473-137-2 **$15.99**

Spiritual Manifestos: Visions for Renewed Religious Life in America from Young
Spiritual Leaders of Many Faiths *Edited by Niles Elliot Goldstein; Preface by Martin E. Marty*
6 x 9, 256 pp, HC, 978-1-893361-09-6 **$21.95**

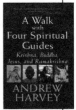

A Walk with Four Spiritual Guides: Krishna, Buddha, Jesus, and Ramakrishna
by Andrew Harvey 5½ x 8½, 192 pp, 10 b/w photos & illus.,Quality PB, 978-1-59473-138-9 **$15.99**

What Matters: Spiritual Nourishment for Head and Heart
by Frederick Franck 5 x 7¼, 128 pp, 50+ b/w illus., HC, 978-1-59473-013-9 **$16.99**

Who Is My God?, 2nd Edition: An Innovative Guide to Finding Your Spiritual Identity
Created by the Editors at SkyLight Paths 6 x 9, 160 pp, Quality PB, 978-1-59473-014-6 **$15.99**

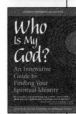

Spirituality—A Week Inside

Come and Sit: A Week Inside Meditation Centers
by Marcia Z. Nelson; Foreword by Wayne Teasdale
The insider's guide to meditation in a variety of different spiritual traditions—
Buddhist, Hindu, Christian, Jewish, and Sufi traditions.
6 x 9, 224 pp, b/w photos, Quality PB, 978-1-893361-35-5 **$16.95**

Lighting the Lamp of Wisdom: A Week Inside a Yoga Ashram
by John Ittner; Foreword by Dr. David Frawley
This insider's guide to Hindu spiritual life takes you into a typical week of retreat
inside a yoga ashram to demystify the experience and show you what to expect.
6 x 9, 192 pp, 10+ b/w photos, Quality PB, 978-1-893361-52-2 **$15.95**

Making a Heart for God: A Week Inside a Catholic Monastery
by Dianne Aprile; Foreword by Brother Patrick Hart, ocso
Takes you to the Abbey of Gethsemani—the Trappist monastery in Kentucky
that was home to author Thomas Merton—to explore the details.
6 x 9, 224 pp, b/w photos, Quality PB, 978-1-893361-49-2 **$16.95**

Waking Up: A Week Inside a Zen Monastery
by Jack Maguire; Foreword by John Daido Loori, Roshi
An essential guide to what it's like to spend a week inside a Zen Buddhist monastery.
6 x 9, 224 pp, b/w photos, Quality PB, 978-1-893361-55-3 **$16.95**
HC, 978-1-893361-13-3 **$21.95**

Fiction / Folktales

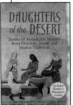

Abraham's Bind & Other Bible Tales of Trickery, Folly, Mercy and Love by Michael J. Caduto
New retellings of episodes in the lives of familiar biblical characters explore relevant life lessons.
6 x 9, 224 pp, HC, 978-1-59473-186-0 **$19.99**

Daughters of the Desert: Stories of Remarkable Women from Christian, Jewish and Muslim Traditions by Claire Rudolf Murphy, Meghan Nuttall Sayres, Mary Cronk Farrell, Sarah Conover and Betsy Wharton
Breathes new life into the old tales of our female ancestors in faith. Uses traditional scriptural passages as starting points, then with vivid detail fills in historical context and place. Chapters reveal the voices of Sarah, Hagar, Huldah, Esther, Salome, Mary Magdalene, Lydia, Khadija, Fatima and many more. Historical fiction ideal for readers of all ages. Quality paperback includes reader's discussion guide.
5½ x 8½, 192 pp, Quality PB, 978-1-59473-106-8 **$14.99**
HC, 192 pp, 978-1-893361-72-0 **$19.95**

The Triumph of Eve & Other Subversive Bible Tales
by Matt Biers-Ariel
Many people were taught and remember only a one-dimensional Bible. These engaging retellings are the antidote to this—they're witty, often hilarious, always profound, and invite you to grapple with questions and issues that are often hidden in the original text.
5½ x 8½, 192 pp, Quality PB, 978-1-59473-176-1 **$14.99**
HC, 192 pp, 978-1-59473-040-5 **$19.99**

Also avail.: **The Triumph of Eve Teacher's Guide**
8½ x 11, 44 pp, PB, 978-1-59473-152-5 **$8.99**

Wisdom in the Telling
Finding Inspiration and Grace in Traditional Folktales and Myths Retold
by Lorraine Hartin-Gelardi
6 x 9, 224 pp, HC, 978-1-59473-185-3 **$19.99**

Religious Etiquette / Reference

How to Be a Perfect Stranger, 4th Edition: The Essential Religious Etiquette Handbook Edited by Stuart M. Matlins and Arthur J. Magida
The indispensable guidebook to help the well-meaning guest when visiting other people's religious ceremonies. A straightforward guide to the rituals and celebrations of the major religions and denominations in the United States and Canada from the perspective of an interested guest of any other faith, based on information obtained from authorities of each religion. Belongs in every living room, library and office. Covers:
African American Methodist Churches • Assemblies of God • Bahá'í • Baptist • Buddhist • Christian Church (Disciples of Christ) • Christian Science (Church of Christ, Scientist) • Churches of Christ • Episcopalian and Anglican • Hindu • Islam • Jehovah's Witnesses • Jewish • Lutheran • Mennonite/Amish • Methodist • Mormon (Church of Jesus Christ of Latter-day Saints) • Native American/First Nations • Orthodox Churches • Pentecostal Church of God • Presbyterian • Quaker (Religious Society of Friends) • Reformed Church in America/Canada • Roman Catholic • Seventh-day Adventist • Sikh • Unitarian Universalist • United Church of Canada • United Church of Christ
6 x 9, 432 pp, Quality PB, 978-1-59473-140-2 **$19.99**

The Perfect Stranger's Guide to Funerals and Grieving Practices: A Guide to Etiquette in Other People's Religious Ceremonies Edited by Stuart M. Matlins
6 x 9, 240 pp, Quality PB, 978-1-893361-20-1 **$16.95**

The Perfect Stranger's Guide to Wedding Ceremonies: A Guide to Etiquette in Other People's Religious Ceremonies Edited by Stuart M. Matlins
6 x 9, 208 pp, Quality PB, 978-1-893361-19-5 **$16.95**

Meditation / Prayer

Prayers to an Evolutionary God
by William Cleary; Afterword by Diarmuid O'Murchu

How is it possible to pray when God is dislocated from heaven, dispersed all around us, and more of a creative force than an all-knowing father? Inspired by the spiritual and scientific teachings of Diarmuid O'Murchu and Teilhard de Chardin, Cleary reveals that religion and science can be combined to create an expanding view of the universe—an evolutionary faith.

6 x 9, 208 pp, HC, 978-1-59473-006-1 **$21.99**

Psalms: A Spiritual Commentary
by M. Basil Pennington, ocso; Illustrations by Phillip Ratner

Showing how the Psalms give profound and candid expression to both our highest aspirations and our deepest pain, the late, highly respected Cistercian Abbot M. Basil Pennington shares his reflections on some of the most beloved passages from the Bible's most widely read book.

6 x 9, 176 pp, HC, 24 full-page b/w illus., 978-1-59473-141-9 **$19.99**

The Song of Songs: A Spiritual Commentary
by M. Basil Pennington, OCSO; Illustrations by Phillip Ratner

Join the late M. Basil Pennington as he ruminates on the Bible's most challenging mystical text. Follow a path into the Songs that weaves through his inspired words and the evocative drawings of Jewish artist Phillip Ratner—a path that reveals your own humanity and leads to the deepest delight of your soul.

6 x 9, 160 pp, HC, 14 b/w illus., 978-1-59473-004-7 **$19.99**

Women of Color Pray: Voices of Strength, Faith, Healing, Hope and Courage   *Edited and with Introductions by Christal M. Jackson*

Through these prayers, poetry, lyrics, meditations and affirmations, you will share in the strong and undeniable connection women of color share with God. It will challenge you to explore new ways of prayerful expression.

5 x 7¼, 208 pp, Quality PB, 978-1-59473-077-1 **$15.99**

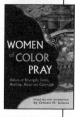

The Art of Public Prayer: Not for Clergy Only
by Lawrence A. Hoffman

An ecumenical resource for all people looking to change hardened worship patterns.

6 x 9, 288 pp, Quality PB, 978-1-893361-06-5 **$18.99**

Finding Grace at the Center, 3rd Ed.: The Beginning of Centering Prayer
by M. Basil Pennington, ocso, Thomas Keating, ocso, and Thomas E. Clarke, sj   Foreword by Rev. Cynthia Bourgeault, PhD

5 x 7¼, 128 pp, Quality PB, 978-1-59473-182-2 **$12.99**

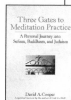

A Heart of Stillness: A Complete Guide to Learning the Art of Meditation
by David A. Cooper   5½ x 8½, 272 pp, Quality PB, 978-1-893361-03-4 **$16.95**

Meditation without Gurus: A Guide to the Heart of Practice
by Clark Strand   5½ x 8½, 192 pp, Quality PB, 978-1-893361-93-5 **$16.95**

Praying with Our Hands: 21 Practices of Embodied Prayer from the World's Spiritual Traditions   *by Jon M. Sweeney; Photographs by Jennifer J. Wilson; Foreword by Mother Tessa Bielecki; Afterword by Taitetsu Unno, PhD*

8 x 8, 96 pp, 22 duotone photos, Quality PB, 978-1-893361-16-4 **$16.95**

Silence, Simplicity & Solitude: A Complete Guide to Spiritual Retreat at Home
by David A. Cooper   5½ x 8½, 336 pp, Quality PB, 978-1-893361-04-1 **$16.95**

Three Gates to Meditation Practice: A Personal Journey into Sufism, Buddhism, and Judaism   *by David A. Cooper*   5½ x 8½, 240 pp, Quality PB, 978-1-893361-22-5 **$16.95**

Women Pray: Voices through the Ages, from Many Faiths, Cultures and Traditions
Edited and with Introductions by Monica Furlong

5 x 7¼, 256 pp, Quality PB, 978-1-59473-071-9 **$15.99**
Deluxe HC with ribbon marker, 978-1-893361-25-6 **$19.95**

Spiritual Biography—SkyLight Lives

SkyLight Lives reintroduces the lives and works of key spiritual figures of our time—people who by their teaching or example have challenged our assumptions about spirituality and have caused us to look at it in new ways.

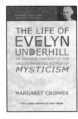 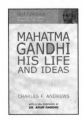 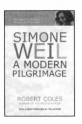 

The Life of Evelyn Underhill
An Intimate Portrait of the Groundbreaking Author of *Mysticism*
by Margaret Cropper; Foreword by Dana Greene
Evelyn Underhill was a passionate writer and teacher who wrote elegantly on mysticism, worship, and devotional life.
6 x 9, 288 pp, 5 b/w photos, Quality PB, 978-1-893361-70-6 **$18.95**

Mahatma Gandhi: His Life and Ideas
by Charles F. Andrews; Foreword by Dr. Arun Gandhi
Examines from a contemporary Christian activist's point of view the religious ideas and political dynamics that influenced the birth of the peaceful resistance movement.
6 x 9, 336 pp, 5 b/w photos, Quality PB, 978-1-893361-89-8 **$18.95**

Simone Weil: A Modern Pilgrimage
by Robert Coles
The extraordinary life of the spiritual philosopher who's been called both saint and madwoman.
6 x 9, 208 pp, Quality PB, 978-1-893361-34-8 **$16.95**

Zen Effects: The Life of Alan Watts
by Monica Furlong
Through his widely popular books and lectures, Alan Watts (1915–1973) did more to introduce Eastern philosophy and religion to Western minds than any figure before or since.
6 x 9, 264 pp, Quality PB, 978-1-893361-32-4 **$16.95**

More Spiritual Biography

Bede Griffiths: An Introduction to His Interspiritual Thought
by Wayne Teasdale
The first study of his contemplative experience and thought, exploring the intersection of Hinduism and Christianity.
6 x 9, 288 pp, Quality PB, 978-1-893361-77-5 **$18.95**

The Soul of the Story: Meetings with Remarkable People
by Rabbi David Zeller
Inspiring and entertaining, this compelling collection of spiritual adventures assures us that no spiritual lesson truly learned is ever lost.
6 x 9, 288 pp, HC, 978-1-58023-272-2 **$21.99** *(a Jewish Lights book)*

Spiritual Poetry—The Mystic Poets

Experience these mystic poets as you never have before. Each beautiful, compact book includes: a brief introduction to the poet's time and place; a summary of the major themes of the poet's mysticism and religious tradition; essential selections from the poet's most important works; and an appreciative preface by a contemporary spiritual writer.

Hafiz: The Mystic Poets
Preface by Ibrahim Gamard

Hafiz is known throughout the world as Persia's greatest poet, with sales of his poems in Iran today only surpassed by those of the Qur'an itself. His probing and joyful verse speaks to people from all backgrounds who long to taste and feel divine love and experience harmony with all living things.

5 x 7¼, 144 pp, HC, 978-1-59473-009-2 **$16.99**

Hopkins: The Mystic Poets
Preface by Rev. Thomas Ryan, CSP

Gerard Manley Hopkins, Christian mystical poet, is beloved for his use of fresh language and startling metaphors to describe the world around him. Although his verse is lovely, beneath the surface lies a searching soul, wrestling with and yearning for God.

5 x 7¼, 112 pp, HC, 978-1-59473-010-8 **$16.99**

Tagore: The Mystic Poets
Preface by Swami Adiswarananda

Rabindranath Tagore is often considered the "Shakespeare" of modern India. A great mystic, Tagore was the teacher of W. B. Yeats and Robert Frost, the close friend of Albert Einstein and Mahatma Gandhi, and the winner of the Nobel Prize for Literature. This beautiful sampling of Tagore's two most important works, *The Gardener* and *Gitanjali,* offers a glimpse into his spiritual vision that has inspired people around the world.

5 x 7¼, 144 pp, HC, 978-1-59473-008-5 **$16.99**

Whitman: The Mystic Poets
Preface by Gary David Comstock

Walt Whitman was the most innovative and influential poet of the nineteenth century. This beautiful sampling of Whitman's most important poetry from *Leaves of Grass,* and selections from his prose writings, offers a glimpse into the spiritual side of his most radical themes— love for country, love for others, and love of Self.

5 x 7¼, 192 pp, HC, 978-1-59473-041-2 **$16.99**

Spirituality & Crafts

The Knitting Way: A Guide to Spiritual Self-Discovery
by Linda Skolnik and Janice MacDaniels
7 x 9, 240 pp, Quality PB, 978-1-59473-079-5 **$16.99**

The Quilting Path
A Guide to Spiritual Discovery through Fabric, Thread and Kabbalah
by Louise Silk
7 x 9, 192 pp, Quality PB, 978-1-59473-206-5 **$16.99**

Spiritual Practice

Divining the Body
Reclaim the Holiness of Your Physical Self *by Jan Phillips*
A practical and inspiring guidebook for connecting the body and soul in spiritual practice. Leads you into a milieu of reverence, mystery and delight, helping you discover your body as a pathway to the Divine.
8 x 8, 256 pp, Quality PB, 978-1-59473-080-1 **$16.99**

Finding Time for the Timeless: Spirituality in the Workweek
by John McQuiston II
Simple, refreshing stories that provide you with examples of how you can refocus and enrich your daily life using prayer or meditation, ritual and other forms of spiritual practice. 5½ x 6¾, 208 pp, HC, 978-1-59473-035-1 **$17.99**

The Gospel of Thomas: A Guidebook for Spiritual Practice
by Ron Miller; Translations by Stevan Davies
An innovative guide to bring a new spiritual classic into daily life.
6 x 9, 160 pp, Quality PB, 978-1-59473-047-4 **$14.99**

Earth, Water, Fire, and Air: Essential Ways of Connecting to Spirit
by Cait Johnson 6 x 9, 224 pp, HC, 978-1-893361-65-2 **$19.95**

Labyrinths from the Outside In: Walking to Spiritual Insight—A Beginner's Guide
by Donna Schaper and Carole Ann Camp
6 x 9, 208 pp, b/w illus. and photos, Quality PB, 978-1-893361-18-8 **$16.95**

Practicing the Sacred Art of Listening: A Guide to Enrich Your Relationships and Kindle Your Spiritual Life—The Listening Center Workshop
by Kay Lindahl 8 x 8, 176 pp, Quality PB, 978-1-893361-85-0 **$16.95**

Releasing the Creative Spirit: Unleash the Creativity in Your Life
by Dan Wakefield 7 x 10, 256 pp, Quality PB, 978-1-893361-36-2 **$16.95**

The Sacred Art of Bowing: Preparing to Practice
by Andi Young 5½ x 8½, 128 pp, b/w illus., Quality PB, 978-1-893361-82-9 **$14.95**

The Sacred Art of Chant: Preparing to Practice
by Ana Hernández 5½ x 8½, 192 pp, Quality PB, 978-1-59473-036-8 **$15.99**

The Sacred Art of Fasting: Preparing to Practice
by Thomas Ryan, CSP 5½ x 8½, 192 pp, Quality PB, 978-1-59473-078-8 **$15.99**

The Sacred Art of Forgiveness: Forgiving Ourselves and Others through God's Grace
by Marcia Ford 8 x 8, 176 pp, Quality PB, 978-1-59473-175-4 **$16.99**

The Sacred Art of Listening: Forty Reflections for Cultivating a Spiritual Practice
by Kay Lindahl; Illustrations by Amy Schnapper
8 x 8, 160 pp, b/w illus., Quality PB, 978-1-893361-44-7 **$16.99**

The Sacred Art of Lovingkindness: Preparing to Practice
by Rabbi Rami Shapiro; Foreword by Marcia Ford
5½ x 8½, 176 pp, Quality PB, 978-1-59473-151-8 **$16.99**

Sacred Speech: A Practical Guide for Keeping Spirit in Your Speech
by Rev. Donna Schaper 6 x 9, 176 pp, Quality PB, 978-1-59473-068-9 **$15.99**
HC, 978-1-893361-74-4 **$21.95**

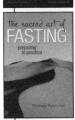

Spirituality of the Seasons

Autumn: A Spiritual Biography of the Season
Edited by Gary Schmidt and Susan M. Felch; Illustrations by Mary Azarian
Rejoice in autumn as a time of preparation and reflection. Includes Wendell Berry, David James Duncan, Robert Frost, A. Bartlett Giamatti, E. B. White, P. D. James, Julian of Norwich, Garret Keizer, Tracy Kidder, Anne Lamott, May Sarton.
6 x 9, 320 pp, 5 b/w illus., Quality PB, 978-1-59473-118-1 **$18.99**
HC, 978-1-59473-005-4 **$22.99**

Spring: A Spiritual Biography of the Season
Edited by Gary Schmidt and Susan M. Felch; Illustrations by Mary Azarian
Explore the gentle unfurling of spring and reflect on how nature celebrates rebirth and renewal. Includes Jane Kenyon, Lucy Larcom, Harry Thurston, Nathaniel Hawthorne, Noel Perrin, Annie Dillard, Martha Ballard, Barbara Kingsolver, Dorothy Wordsworth, Donald Hall, David Brill, Lionel Basney, Isak Dinesen, Paul Laurence Dunbar.
6 x 9, 352 pp, 6 b/w illus., HC, 978-1-59473-114-3 **$21.99**

Summer: A Spiritual Biography of the Season
Edited by Gary Schmidt and Susan M. Felch; Illustrations by Barry Moser
"A sumptuous banquet.... These selections lift up an exquisite wholeness found within an everyday sophistication." — ★ *Publishers Weekly* starred review
Includes Anne Lamott, Luci Shaw, Ray Bradbury, Richard Selzer, Thomas Lynch, Walt Whitman, Carl Sandburg, Sherman Alexie, Madeleine L'Engle, Jamaica Kincaid.
6 x 9, 304 pp, 5 b/w illus., HC, 978-1-59473-083-2 **$21.99**

Winter: A Spiritual Biography of the Season
Edited by Gary Schmidt and Susan M. Felch; Illustrations by Barry Moser
"This outstanding anthology features top-flight nature and spirituality writers on the fierce, inexorable season of winter.... Remarkably lively and warm, despite the icy subject." — ★ *Publishers Weekly* starred review.
Includes Will Campbell, Rachel Carson, Annie Dillard, Donald Hall, Ron Hansen, Jane Kenyon, Jamaica Kincaid, Barry Lopez, Kathleen Norris, John Updike, E. B. White.
6 x 9, 288 pp, 6 b/w illus., Deluxe PB w/flaps, 978-1-893361-92-8 **$18.95**
HC, 978-1-893361-53-9 **$21.95**

Spirituality / Animal Companions

Blessing the Animals: Prayers and Ceremonies to Celebrate God's Creatures, Wild and Tame   *Edited by Lynn L. Caruso*   5 x 7¼, 256 pp, HC, 978-1-59473-145-7 **$19.99**

What Animals Can Teach Us about Spirituality: Inspiring Lessons from Wild and Tame Creatures   *by Diana L. Guerrero*   6 x 9, 176 pp, Quality PB, 978-1-893361-84-3 **$16.95**

Spirituality

Awakening the Spirit, Inspiring the Soul
30 Stories of Interspiritual Discovery in the Community of Faiths
Edited by Brother Wayne Teasdale and Martha Howard, MD; Foreword by Joan Borysenko, PhD
Thirty original spiritual mini-autobiographies showcase the varied ways that people come to faith—and what that means—in today's multi-religious world.
6 x 9, 224 pp, HC, 978-1-59473-039-9 **$21.99**

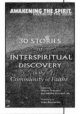

The Alphabet of Paradise: An A–Z of Spirituality for Everyday Life
by Howard Cooper   5 x 7¼, 224 pp, Quality PB, 978-1-893361-80-5 **$16.95**

Creating a Spiritual Retirement: A Guide to the Unseen Possibilities in Our Lives
by Molly Srode   6 x 9, 208 pp, b/w photos, Quality PB, 978-1-59473-050-4 **$14.99**
HC, 978-1-893361-75-1 **$19.95**

Finding Hope: Cultivating God's Gift of a Hopeful Spirit
by Marcia Ford   8 x 8, 200 pp, Quality PB, 978-1-59473-211-9 **$16.99**

The Geography of Faith: Underground Conversations on Religious, Political and Social Change   *by Daniel Berrigan and Robert Coles*   6 x 9, 224 pp, Quality PB, 978-1-893361-40-9 **$16.95**

God Within: Our Spiritual Future—As Told by Today's New Adults   *Edited by Jon M. Sweeney and the Editors at SkyLight Paths*   6 x 9, 176 pp, Quality PB, 978-1-893361-15-7 **$14.95**

Sacred Texts—SkyLight Illuminations Series

Offers today's spiritual seeker an accessible entry into the great classic texts of the world's spiritual traditions. Each classic is presented in an accessible translation with facing pages of guided commentary from experts, giving you the keys you need to understand the history, context and meaning of the text. This series enables you, whatever your background, to experience and understand classic spiritual texts directly, and to make them a part of your life.

CHRISTIANITY

The End of Days: Essential Selections from Apocalyptic Texts—
Annotated & Explained *Annotation by Robert G. Clouse*
Helps you understand the complex Christian visions of the end of the world.
5½ x 8½, 224 pp, Quality PB, 978-1-59473-170-9 **$16.99**

The Hidden Gospel of Matthew: Annotated & Explained
Translation & Annotation by Ron Miller
Takes you deep into the text cherished around the world to discover the words and events that have the strongest connection to the historical Jesus.
5½ x 8½, 272 pp, Quality PB, 978-1-59473-038-2 **$16.99**

The Lost Sayings of Jesus: Teachings from Ancient Christian, Jewish, Gnostic and Islamic Sources—Annotated & Explained
Translation & Annotation by Andrew Phillip Smith; Foreword by Stephan A. Hoeller
This collection of more than three hundred sayings depicts Jesus as a Wisdom teacher who speaks to people of all faiths as a mystic and spiritual master.
5½ x 8½, 240 pp, Quality PB, 978-1-59473-172-3 **$16.99**

Philokalia: The Eastern Christian Spiritual Texts—Selections Annotated & Explained *Annotation by Allyne Smith; Translation by G. E. H. Palmer, Phillip Sherrard and Bishop Kallistos Ware*
The first approachable introduction to the wisdom of the Philokalia, which is the classic text of Eastern Christian spirituality.
5½ x 8½, 240 pp, Quality PB, 978-1-59473-103-7 **$16.99**

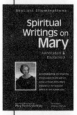

Spiritual Writings on Mary: Annotated & Explained
Annotation by Mary Ford-Grabowsky; Foreword by Andrew Harvey
Examines the role of Mary, the mother of Jesus, as a source of inspiration in history and in life today. 5½ x 8½, 288 pp, Quality PB, 978-1-59473-001-6 **$16.99**

The Way of a Pilgrim: Annotated & Explained
Translation & Annotation by Gleb Pokrovsky; Foreword by Andrew Harvey
This classic of Russian spirituality is the delightful account of one man who sets out to learn the prayer of the heart, also known as the "Jesus prayer."
5½ x 8½, 160 pp, Illus., Quality PB, 978-1-893361-31-7 **$14.95**

MORMONISM

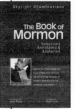

The Book of Mormon: Selections Annotated & Explained
Annotation by Jana Riess; Foreword by Phyllis Tickle
Explores the sacred epic that is cherished by more than twelve million members of the LDS church as the keystone of their faith.
5½ x 8½ , 272 pp, Quality PB, 978-1-59473-076-4 **$16.99**

NATIVE AMERICAN

Native American Stories of the Sacred: Annotated & Explained
Retold & Annotated by Evan T. Pritchard
Intended for more than entertainment, these teaching tales contain elegantly simple illustrations of time-honored truths.
5½ x 8½, 272 pp, Quality PB, 978-1-59473-112-9 **$16.99**

Sacred Texts—cont.

GNOSTICISM

The Gospel of Philip: Annotated & Explained
Translation & Annotation by Andrew Phillip Smith; Foreword by Stevan Davies
Reveals otherwise unrecorded sayings of Jesus and fragments of Gnostic mythology.
½ x 8½, 160 pp, Quality PB, 978-1-59473-111-2 **$16.99**

The Gospel of Thomas: Annotated & Explained
Translation & Annotation by Stevan Davies Sheds new light on the origins of Christianity and portrays Jesus as a wisdom-loving sage. 5½ x 8½, 192 pp, Quality PB, 978-1-893361-45-4 **$16.99**

The Secret Book of John: The Gnostic Gospel—Annotated & Explained
Translation & Annotation by Stevan Davies The most significant and influential text of the ancient Gnostic religion. 5½ x 8½, 208 pp, Quality PB, 978-1-59473-082-5 **$16.99**

JUDAISM

The Divine Feminine in Biblical Wisdom Literature
Selections Annotated & Explained
Translation & Annotation by Rabbi Rami Shapiro; Foreword by Rev. Cynthia Bourgeault, PhD
Uses the Hebrew books of Psalms, Proverbs, Song of Songs, Ecclesiastes and Job, Wisdom literature and the Wisdom of Solomon to clarify who Wisdom is.
½ x 8½, 240 pp, Quality PB, 978-1-59473-109-9 **$16.99**

Ethics of the Sages: *Pirke Avot*—Annotated & Explained
Translation & Annotation by Rabbi Rami Shapiro Clarifies the ethical teachings of the early Rabbis. 5½ x 8½, 192 pp, Quality PB, 978-1-59473-207-2 **$16.99**

Hasidic Tales: Annotated & Explained
Translation & Annotation by Rabbi Rami Shapiro
Introduces the legendary tales of the impassioned Hasidic rabbis, presenting them as stories rather than as parables. 5½ x 8½, 240 pp, Quality PB, 978-1-893361-86-7 **$16.95**

The Hebrew Prophets: Selections Annotated & Explained
Translation & Annotation by Rabbi Rami Shapiro; Foreword by Zalman M. Schachter-Shalomi
Focuses on the central themes covered by all the Hebrew prophets.
½ x 8½, 224 pp, Quality PB, 978-1-59473-037-5 **$16.99**

Zohar: Annotated & Explained *Translation & Annotation by Daniel C. Matt*
The best-selling author of *The Essential Kabbalah* brings together in one place the most important teachings of the Zohar, the canonical text of Jewish mystical tradition.
½ x 8½, 176 pp, Quality PB, 978-1-893361-51-5 **$15.99**

EASTERN RELIGIONS

Bhagavad Gita: Annotated & Explained *Translation by Shri Purohit Swami*
Annotation by Kendra Crossen Burroughs Explains references and philosophical terms, shares the interpretations of famous spiritual leaders and scholars, and more.
½ x 8½, 192 pp, Quality PB, 978-1-893361-28-7 **$16.95**

Dhammapada: Annotated & Explained *Translation by Max Müller and revised by Jack Maguire; Annotation by Jack Maguire* Contains all of Buddhism's key teachings.
½ x 8½, 160 pp, b/w photos, Quality PB, 978-1-893361-42-3 **$14.95**

Rumi and Islam: Selections from His Stories, Poems, and Discourses—
Annotated & Explained *Translation & Annotation by Ibrahim Gamard*
Focuses on Rumi's place within the Sufi tradition of Islam, providing insight into the mystical side of the religion. 5½ x 8½, 240 pp, Quality PB, 978-1-59473-002-3 **$15.99**

Selections from the Gospel of Sri Ramakrishna: Annotated & Explained
Translation by Swami Nikhilananda; Annotation by Kendra Crossen Burroughs
Introduces the fascinating world of the Indian mystic and the universal appeal of his message. 5½ x 8½, 240 pp, b/w photos, Quality PB, 978-1-893361-46-1 **$16.95**

Tao Te Ching: Annotated & Explained *Translation & Annotation by Derek Lin*
Foreword by Lama Surya Das Introduces an Eastern classic in an accessible, poetic and completely original way. 5½ x 8½, 192 pp, Quality PB, 978-1-59473-204-1 **$16.99**

AVAILABLE FROM BETTER BOOKSTORES.
TRY YOUR BOOKSTORE FIRST.

About SKYLIGHT PATHS Publishing

SkyLight Paths Publishing is creating a place where people of different spiritual traditions come together for challenge and inspiration, a place where we can help each other understand the mystery that lies at the heart of our existence.

Through spirituality, our religious beliefs are increasingly becoming a part of our lives—rather than *apart* from our lives. While many of us may be more interested than ever in spiritual growth, we may be less firmly planted in traditional religion. Yet, we do want to deepen our relationship to the sacred, to learn from our own as well as from other faith traditions, and to practice in new ways.

SkyLight Paths sees both believers and seekers as a community that increasingly transcends traditional boundaries of religion and denomination—people wanting to learn from each other, *walking together, finding the way.*

For your information and convenience, at the back of this book we have provided a list of other SkyLight Paths books you might find interesting and useful. They cover the following subjects:

Buddhism / Zen	Gnosticism	Mysticism
Catholicism	Hinduism /	Poetry
Children's Books	Vedanta	Prayer
Christianity	Inspiration	Religious Etiquette
Comparative	Islam / Sufism	Retirement
Religion	Judaism / Kabbalah /	Spiritual Biography
Current Events	Enneagram	Spiritual Direction
Earth-Based	Meditation	Spirituality
Spirituality	Midrash Fiction	Women's Interest
Global Spiritual	Monasticism	Worship
Perspectives		

Or phone, fax, mail or e-mail to: SKYLIGHT PATHS Publishing
Sunset Farm Offices, Route 4 • P.O. Box 237 • Woodstock, Vermont 05091
Tel: (802) 457-4000 • Fax: (802) 457-4004 • www.skylightpaths.com
Credit card orders: (800) 962-4544 (8:30AM–5:30PM ET Monday–Friday)
Generous discounts on quantity orders. SATISFACTION GUARANTEED. Prices subject to change.

For more information about each book,
visit our website at www.skylightpaths.com